The 80/20 Business

By Todd W. Nuckols

This publication is designed to provide accurate and authoritative information in regard to the subject matter covered. It is sold with the understanding that neither the author nor publisher is engaged in rendering legal or accounting services. If legal advice or other expert assistance is required, the services of a competent professional person should be sought.

DEDICATION

Mom & Dad, whether I wanted to be a magician, a baseball player or an astronaut you always said *"go for it!"* I couldn't have done this without your love and support.

Table of Contents

What is 80/20 and why is it important?

Since Vilfredo Pareto started making observations about Italian land owners in the early 1900s, the Pareto Principle, or 80/20 rule, has been investigated and applied in all facets of life. In Pareto's observations he discovered that 80% or more of the wealth was held by 20% of the population. But, after further investigation it didn't stop there.

The maxim that 20% of our activities give us 80% of our results holds true time and time again; it's a state of nature. While we can try hard to fight it, we can't escape it.

However, this book is not about "finding your 20%." Instead, what I am going to show you is that the 20% really doesn't matter at all. In fact, it's the 80/20 *within* the 20% that matters.

Mathematically that means as little as 5% of your activities will produce as much as 50% (or more) of your results.

Let's take a look at a few real world examples. For the golfers out there you already know that the typical golfer carries FOURTEEN golf clubs in their bag. You also know that a typical round of golf is designed to take 72 strokes or swings. What you also know is that there is ONE club designed to be used 36 of those 72 strokes. What is it? Well, it's the putter of course! A typical putter should be used 50% (or more) of the time depending on your level of golfing talent.

On the flip side there is one club that all golfers spend the majority of their practice time using. What is that? Well, it's the driver of course! Why the driver? Well, the golfer's ego always wants to hit the ball well off the tee and they want to look good to their playing partners. So, how many times is the driver designed to be used in a typical round of golf? It should be used no more than fourteen times out of 72 total strokes.

Now let's look at the math behind this. One club (the putter) is used at least 50% of the time. This one club represents 1 out of 14 total clubs or about 7% of the total clubs in your bag. This is not only a great example of how the 80/20 within the 20% works but it also shows you that 5% is a floating average and 7% is okay too.

What about the driver? Well, it too represents only 7% of the clubs in the bag and it is designed to be used only 19% of the time during a round of golf. But, how much practice time does the typical golfer devote to the driver? If I said 90% I would not be exaggerating because most golfers devote ALL of their time to this one club.

The point of this story is to show how we can focus our energies on items that give us little in return. For the golfer, if they spent 50% or more of their time practicing on the putting green their scores would decrease and they would be much happier. But why don't they do that? Because it's not as energetic as hitting the driver a long way and furthermore, most golfers are playing for fun and not competition. If they truly wanted to compete they would do what professionals do and practice their putting a great deal of the time. This is a symptom of our human nature and it passes over to our business habits as well.

If golf is not your sport then you can apply the 80/20 within the 20% to something that all of us are familiar with – *watching television*. In today's world we each have access to 200+ channels with the click of our remote. But, how many of those channels do we actually watch? When I tested this on my own viewing habits I found that 90% of my television watching occurred on fewer than ten channels. Mathematically that means 5% or less of the channels were responsible for 90% of my viewing time. It also means there were 190+ channels that I rarely if ever saw during a viewing month, but I still paid for! I'm sure the same applies to you as well.

If you think about it further you will find many more examples of the 80/20 within the 20% that apply to your life every day.

Don't believe me?

Keep reading because I'm not only going to show you how that happens, but I'm going to show you specifically how to apply this concept to your business, your sales team, your life and more.

The principles I will teach you, when applied, will allow you to accomplish so much more in so much less time it will make your head spin.

But don't take my word for it. Instead, take it as a challenge to apply what follows in this book for at least 30 days and then see if you want to go back to your old way of doing things.

Since the year 2000 I have consulted for over 500 businesses in 35 states and two countries. I've interviewed close to 1,000 business owners and probably 5,000+ workers.

I asked questions such as:

If you could change something about your situation what would you change?

What do you like about what you do?

What do you dislike about what you do?

Do you know how each interviewee responded time and time again? They always, and I mean always, gave me no more than three items as an answer to each question. And, many times they only gave me ONE.

I look at this as 80/20 in a different way but my point is this: there are not 100 problems that businesses need fixed. Instead, there are really only a few. If you could identify those three to five items and actually take steps to fix them, how much better would your business be?

Whether you are looking to become a better leader, increase your sales, or plan for the future, the 80/20 rule will apply. And once you figure out the 5% within each area of your business, you'll be ready to make the most important, impactful, and necessary changes in your operation.

What does an 80/20 business look like?

If you are like most business owners, you have been open for 5 years or more. During that time you have probably faced many ups and downs.

When things were not working well, perhaps you struggled to figure out why.

When things were going great, you might have chalked it up to "pure luck."

Now I'm not saying luck never plays a role in business because I've seen that it does time and time again. Rather, I'm saying that you can *create more luck* in your life by doing the RIGHT things more often than the WRONG things.

If you walked into a perfect "80/20 Business" you would observe several things immediately.

The first thing you would notice is the leader of the business actively applies the traits that all great leaders exhibit. These traits could be as simple as making workers feel important, treating them like humans (and not just workers) and being consistent in how all workers are treated. But, every leader is different and I'm going to let you figure out your personal list of leadership traits later on in the book. But remember, it all starts with the leader!

The next thing you would observe is an 80/20 staff that is trying hard to focus on those two to three items that make them better, which in turn makes the business better. Are they perfect? No. Do they accomplish more in less time. Absolutely!

Believe it or not, workers expand or contract based on how much time is given to a specific task. If they have eight hours to do the task they will often take eight hours. If they have two hours to complete the task how long do you think it will take?

Yeah, you guessed it . . . two hours!

This is called Parkinson's Law and it's part of our human nature. If workers are going to fill their work day anyway, wouldn't it be better to have them spend their time on the 5% of activities that matter the most?

From a sales perspective, an 80/20 business would first and foremost have a solid sales funnel. This means that leads drop in the top of the funnel and a percentage of them pop out at the bottom as new customers. This sales funnel would be systematically designed based on what has worked best for YOU in the past. (We'll work on developing your personal 80/20 activity list later in the book.)

Finally, all great businesses must plan for their future. But where do you begin?

I'll give you a hint. If 5% of your customers (or customer types) produce 50% of your sales, wouldn't it make sense to use them as a model for the future? Of course it would!

By completing this book you will have your personal blueprint for leadership, sales and future planning that gives you the greatest chance of success.

The bottom line is that a true "80/20 Business" is a well-oiled machine where all parts are working towards a common goal. It is not perfect and it never will be. In business, "stuff" happens all of the time that is completely outside of our control.

But, by focusing on the 5% of tasks that matter, you give your business the best shot for success year after year.

Prepare for the unknown now and you are more likely to survive and thrive – while your competition falters.

Becoming an 80/20 Leader

We have all had 80/20 leaders in our life. These are the men and women who made a difference and inspired us to reach higher day after day. They just seemed to do and say the "right things" day in and day out, without fail.

To be sure, these leaders and role models weren't 100% perfect (nobody is!), but they seemed to do more right than wrong and they created a track record of consistency which meant you trusted what they said, and what they would do in the future.

Now let's flip the table and think about the BAD leaders we all have had in our lives. The bad ones probably stand out in our memory more than the good ones because human nature is to avoid pain at all costs, and we certainly know what we *don't want* in a boss. These leaders consistently did the WRONG things, created a track record of mistrust, and quite often we dreaded facing them each day.

So, was it luck that the first leader was so much better than the second leader in this example? No, it wasn't luck at all. Instead it was a habit they developed over their lifetime.

Whether it was conscious or not, these leaders were actively exhibiting (or avoiding) the 5% of actions that made the biggest positive impact.

Think about it for a minute and write down three to five things that the GOOD leader(s) in your life exhibited that made you feel they were good leaders.

1

2.

3.

4.

5.

Did you get to five DIFFERENT habits?

Many people don't get past three and then struggle to go further; that in itself proves that it's not the 20% of what we do that matters but the 5% or less!

Think about this one more time. The person you labeled as "great" consistently did three to five activities, and the end result was a happy workforce and probably a stronger business.

Now, do another exercise and think about the BAD leaders in your life. Did they do ANY of the items you listed above? Probably not at all.

But, the 5% rule still applies and let me prove it to you. Take a minute and write down what the BAD boss did each and every day that made them "BAD" in your mind.

Ready, set, go . . .

1.

2.

3.

4.

5.

Did you write down five DIFFERENT things or did you write down five scenarios that involved SIMILAR actions? If you are like most people, you probably struggled to write down more than three different actions they exhibited that made them "bad."

But, you would have no problem thinking of the myriad examples of how these actions resulted in gloom and doom for all involved.

The bottom line is that GREAT leaders do the same 5% of activities each day that make them great and BAD leaders do the same 5% of activities that make them BAD at their jobs. This proves the theory that SMALL things create BIG results – good or bad.

The important part about having an 80/20 mindset and practicing it each day is the trickle-down effect it has on your staff. You might be familiar with the old adage, "Nobody can care more than the leader," and it is 100% true.

Workers *want to follow* a good leader who has a clear vision and who supports their activities each day. They want someone who will point them in a direction and then get out of their way. They want someone that will guide them back to the path when they get a bit off track. Good leaders do all of this and more.

If you want to become one of these GREAT leaders, it's time to find out what you do each day that matters the most.

On the following page I will guide you through the first of several 80/20 exercises that will result in your personal 5% that makes the biggest difference. Once you have the results, it is up to you to exhibit these qualities each day – no one else can do it for you!

Let's get started . . .

The 80/20 Business Map

Step One: Write down the names of as many GOOD leaders in your life as you can remember:

Step Two: For the next two minutes do a "mind dump" and write out what these leaders did consistently that made them "good."

Step Three: Identify the three to five activities in Step #2 that made the most impact on you personally. Write these down now.

Step Four: Prioritize the list in Step #3 based on the biggest POSITIVE impact those activities had on the workforce.

Step Five: Write down how you are going to *apply* the list in step #4 to YOUR situation. Be as specific as possible about how you are going to take these actions.

Your Personal 80/20 Leadership Map

I _____ will do the following leadership
activities on a consistent basis each day:

1.

2.

3.

4.

5.

Sign: _____

Date: _____

"Finding the 5's"

The key to being a great leader and accomplishing more within your organization than you ever thought possible lies within the tasks you CHOOSE to take on. As the leader, you may have built this company from the ground up, but if you want to turn it into a *business* (and not just "a job"), you must learn to remove tasks from your plate.

If you truly want to get to the next level, you must take time to get into the minutia of what you do each day, week or year. How are you really spending your time?

When I coach business leaders, I use the following exercise to help them "Find the 5's" – the vital few activities that mean the most to them, and that will ultimately lead to the most profit for their business.

Step One: Do a "mind dump" and write out as many activities you "touch" in any given day, week or month.

Don't leave anything out. If "opening the mail" is part of your day then write it down. The more detail the better because we all do so many things on a daily basis that have *no impact* on our business's overall success.

Step Two: Turn the items in Step #1 into a bullet point list of activities.

I prefer to do this in a spreadsheet, and you can download a free copy of the template I use with all of my coaching prospects here:

www.ToddNuckols.com/Resources

The reason I prefer a spreadsheet format is that it will make it easier to sort your activities. Additionally, if you use the form in my resource section you will find it easier to separate your activities into logical categories.

Step Three: Beside each activity, rank these on a scale of 1 to 5, with 5 being the most important. For example, anything that rates a 5 should have a direct, tangible impact on the bottom line. These are the activities that consistently and predictably earn money for the company.

On the other side of the equation, something that rates a 1 might still generate money someday, but there is no direct "cause and effect" to this activity.

Step Four: Highlight all of the "5" activities. These will form the basis of your future actions.

In most situations, you will find these represent 10% or less of your overall activities which aligns perfectly with the 80/20 principles we have discussed so far.

The reality is that there are very few items that contribute to our overall success –but if we just focused on these alone, what would we do to fill our days?

After all, our culture typically rewards "hard work" over "smart work." But, this is YOUR business and this is YOUR workplace culture so you get to choose the bar you set for yourself and your team. By demonstrating "smart work" and requiring it amongst your staff as well, you are building a team of "all stars" that will help you thrive for years to come.

Step Five: This is the hardest step of all because it requires you to make a decision.

You must decide what you will give up on your "to do" list and what you will concentrate on instead. Giving up items means changing your habits – and all of us love our habits because they create comfortable patterns in our lives.

But what is most comfortable is not always most profitable, and if you desire to **"Do More With Less"** then you must ultimately dismiss those tasks that are keeping you from reaching your goal.

In the daily life of a business leader there are many things you COULD do, but it all boils down to two things you SHOULD do. You should:

1. Spend business time doing "5" business activities.
2. Spend personal time doing "5" personal activities.

Again, if we just did this and delegated or outsourced the rest we would make more money than we ever thought possible. The problem is that we spend too much of our time on items less than "5" – and while they fill our days, they don't make us any more money.

Great leaders identify this truth faster than weak leaders, and more importantly, they do something about it.

They hire great workers, they outsource to experts, and they find ways to **"Do More With Less,"** which means less time, fewer full-time workers, less equipment, less business overhead. In other words, they run like a well-oiled machine. This is the future in which we live. Thanks to the Internet and its ability to connect us with the best resources in the world, we can do things with our businesses today that our fathers never thought possible.

BONUS LEADERSHIP TIP:

"If you are the major COG of your business then you are the major CLOG of your business!"

In the life of the business leader there will ALWAYS be times when you are the major COG. Heck, there will be times when you are the ONLY cog in your business!

But as you grow, you must reach out and learn to work through others. This could mean outsourcing what you do but it will always mean working THROUGH (and not against) your staff. THEY are the key to your future success – don't forget it!

How do you stop being the major COG?

Step 1: Grow your business. It sounds simple but it's very difficult and we will discuss proven methods later in this book.

Step 2: Hire great workers. Hire people who are energetic, smart, and have great attitudes. (The attitude part is virtually impossible to train because they either "have it" or they don't.)

THEY decide if they come to work every day with a great attitude. YOU decide if you are going to keep them or not. Bottom line, don't keep bad attitudes . . . they are a cancer to your organization. Later on we will cover this in more detail.

Step 3: Train these workers to do their jobs. Again, it sounds simple but we often take the approach of, "I can do it in 10 minutes or take 30 minutes to train the new worker . . . so I'll just do it myself." That is the PERFECT example of CLOG thinking. Don't fall into that trap!

Step 4: GET OUT OF THE WAY! After scaling up your business, hiring great people, and training them in your systems, it's now up to you as the great and powerful leader to GET OUT OF THE WAY and let your people do their job. The ball is in your court!

The good news is that you will be learning all of this and more as we progress through this book. But it all starts with you.

If you desire a positive change in your entire organization then you must create the positive change in yourself first. Like a boulder perched atop a hill, it will begin to roll only after you give it the initial push. Are you ready to push?

Building an 80/20 Workforce

Building an 80/20 workforce is only possible if the leader and the rest of the management team are on board with 80/20 principles. If they are not, then nothing else matters because "nobody can care more than the leader(s)!" Assuming the leadership team is on board with the principles in the last chapter, the rest becomes much easier.

80/20, like many business management programs, is a "trickle-down" philosophy. This means it starts at the top and flows all the way down until everyone, including the lowest paid worker at your business, strives to act upon the 5% of activities that makes them better at their job.

But here is the catch . . .

Workers are watching you, the leader, to see how serious you are about this!

In the thousands of worker interviews I've conducted I always ask how the worker feels about their boss. And, the two most common complaints I hear are:

1. The top of the organization does a poor job communicating future changes down to us.
2. The only time my boss talks to me is when they need to tell me I've done something wrong.

These two responses have occurred at small AND large businesses alike; human nature doesn't relate the size of your business. It is natural for most leaders to sit in their offices and avoid communicating with their direct reports because that is where they feel most comfortable. What isn't always comfortable is creating a bond with workers who you may have to terminate someday. The thought process is, "If I put up a wall, then they fear me and through that fear they will work harder."

This cannot be further from the truth!

Leaders should be the type of people who not only show a worker the overall vision, but *inspire* the worker to follow them until, as a team, they cross the goal line.

Then, it's the leader's job to create a NEW goal and start the process again!

If you want workers to respond to you in a positive way, you have to continually exhibit the 5% of qualities you discovered in the last section of this book. There is no other way to make this happen! There are no shortcuts on becoming a compassionate human being!

The first thing you need to do to create this positive trickle-down effect in your business is to walk through the exercise at the end of this chapter with every one of your direct reports. I prefer to do this exercise in small groups of no more than 5 workers at a time, but you can certainly do this one-on-one if you prefer.

Also, notice I said to work with only the people that DIRECTLY report to YOU. This is an important step because this is a chance to bond with your team and show them you care. Explain that you have gone through this exercise too and you have things to work on as well.

When the exercise is complete and your team is aware of the actions they must take on a daily basis to make the greatest difference, the work is just beginning for you as the leader!

From this point forward the worker(s) are looking to see if you will back off, change direction or go back to old habits. They know that leaders in their company often come back from a meeting or event with a "new great idea" that will change the world. According to the workers I've interviewed, this is usually nothing more than a two week event before the leader goes back to old, comfortable, habits.

The energy that made you rise up the ranks and become a great leader can be the same energy that sidetracks you as you see the next "shiny thing."

Creating an 80/20 workforce is not easy because you are trying to change people's habits – and humans are prone to stick even to BAD habits out of comfort. In fact, studies have shown that even if people *know* the new habit will make them richer, thinner, or better in any way they STILL often stay in the muck out of fear of change. Or, better yet, out of lack of motivation. How many people buy gym memberships in January and stop going to the gym by February? If the goal we have for ourselves is not something we have a passion about then just about anything will divert us.

As a leader you must be there to start the race and you must be there to encourage everyone along when you see them return to old habits. It won't be easy, but it will change your life (and theirs)!

On the following page is the 80/20 Worker Map. It is designed to help each member of your team identify the daily activities that will make the biggest difference in their work and their life. After each worker completes this exercise make a copy for your records so you can coach them along to the finish line!

The 80/20 Worker Map

Step One: Describe a perfect day at work. What specifically occurs that makes it so perfect?

Step Two: For the next several minutes, write down what needs to happen to recreate that day from the moment you walk in the door to the moment you leave work.

Step Three: Identify the three to five activities in Step #2 that have the greatest impact on you professionally. Write these down now.

Step Four: Prioritize the list in Step #3 based on the biggest perceived impact those activities have on your day.

Step Five: Write down how you are going to apply the list in step #4 to YOUR job. Be as specific as possible about how you are going to take these actions.

Hiring 80/20 Workers

As the 80/20 principles apply to every aspect of our lives, they can be seen quite clearly in the hiring of new workers. First, before you go further, write down a list of your workers or the workers that directly report to you if you happen to run a larger business.

Now, prioritize that list from top to bottom, beginning with your "all-stars" and continuing down to your least productive employees. According to legendary CEO Jack Welch, you can easily get rid of the bottom 10% of your workforce without having an issue. He was right, *and* he was being conservative.

Now I'm not telling you to fire your entire workforce, but I am saying that it takes MUCH LESS than 90% of your current staff to provide excellent results for your customers and drive future growth.

If you are like most business owners who just did this exercise you probably have three to five percent of your workers who are "all-stars". And while (hopefully) the rest are great, they are probably more replaceable than the top 5%.

In fact, if you really analyze that top 5% and their contributions to your business you will most likely find that they:

- Are directly responsible for 50% (or more) of your profits!
- Are directly responsible for 50% (or more) of your sales!
- Are directly responsible for 50% (or more) of your production!
- Are directly responsible for 50% (or more) of your professional happiness!

Statistically this means they are 10 times more important to your business than the other 95%! Shocked? You shouldn't be at this point because you knew where I was going with this. But it is still shocking when you look around your business and realize the tremendous impact only a small percentage of your staff makes.

Now that you know who your "all-stars" are, it is time to define them a little better. Take out a sheet of paper and answer the following questions:

1. What specifically do these workers do during the day that makes them great?

2. How do they handle pressure?

3. How do they treat other workers?

4. How do they treat their superiors?

5. How do they handle customer interaction (if applicable)?

6. How do they handle ANGRY customers (if applicable)?

7. How do they act in group settings (meetings, training, etc.)?

I believe you will start to see patterns emerge as you turn your feelings into facts. Make sure you turn "feeling" words like, "They are great team players," into specific situations such as, "Joe was sick so Mary stepped up to the plate and finished his workload without anyone asking her to."

The more specific you are the better this will be for you when we get to the hiring stage.

Advertising for "All-Star" Workers

Now that you have gone through the exercise of identifying the best qualities of the Top 5% of your workers it's time to find more of them. What do you do with the lesser producing workers? We will get to that in later chapters but for the purpose of this exercise let us focus on the "all stars" on our team. With that in mind, the first "filter" for new team members is the advertisement you use to attract future workers.

Most companies today use online resources for recruiting and I can recommend two: Hyrell.com and Indeed.com. Both are great for getting the word out to a larger base, and when searching for workers the best thing you can do is cast as wide a net as possible.

With your checklist of what makes a great worker in hand, it is time to write the ad. If you want better candidates, you must write better ads. They need to be VERY specific and fill in the gap of what the worker expects and what YOU expect.

Now, this doesn't mean you won't get a few bad resumes; but it does mean you are giving your hiring activities the best chance of success. Here is an example of an ad you can use for your business. Just change everything in bold and you will be ready to get the word out!

COMPANY NAME is currently looking for a **JOB TITLE** to assist in the growth of our dynamic company.

In this role, you will work BE SPECIFIC ON THE DAILY ACTIVITIES. The successful candidate will be comfortable BE SPECIFIC ON THE SKILL SETS THEY SHOULD POSSESS.

This is a hands-on position, with a high level of accountability and you will be judged on **BE SPECIFIC AS TO WHAT YOU EXPECT**.

Additional duties include:

• SPECIFIC DUTY #1

• SPECIFIC DUTY #2

• SPECIFIC DUTY #3

• SPECIFIC DUTY #4

Compensation package is commensurate with experience, but includes a base salary along with performance incentives **(or insert a specific salary)**.

Position is full time. For immediate consideration please include a resume and cover letter that demonstrates your abilities to achieve measurable results.

I know this ad works because I've used it many times myself. The key is to be as specific as possible and to include the EXACT qualities or activities that your "all-star" workers exhibit on a daily basis. Tell the worker / prospect what you expect them to do and it becomes much easier to hold them accountable to your expectations. No surprises.

How to handle those who apply for the job

Once the resumes roll in, it is time to apply the 80/20 principles once again. There is no need in wasting your time on every applicant when only 5% will statistically be potential "all-stars."

The first place to do your 80/20 analysis is with the resume or application itself. Look for whether they meet the criteria you outlined in the advertisement.

This is the first "filter" and if they don't meet ALL criteria then move their resume to the side and put it in a box. I would even go as far as to get rid of the resume all together because not following directions is the first indicator they won't be an "all-star" worker in the future.

The next thing you want to look at is the overall aesthetic form of the resume. Is it professional? Are there typographical errors? All of these are red flags and telltale signs of trouble.

Remember, once you eventually hire a worker they will be the best they will ever be in their first 90 days. I'm not saying they won't improve over time but what I mean is they will put their "best foot forward" in the first 90 days and if they are making small errors now it will only get worse! If they can't put their "best foot forward" while applying for the job then there is little chance they will step up to the challenge once hired!

Once you go through the culling process to eliminate 95% of the resumes that you have received it is time to prioritize them. Remember, there is even an 80/20 within the remaining 5%! So, if you still have more than five applicants at this point I recommend you find the 80/20 within the remaining applicants and get your list down to no more than five.

Why five? Because in my experience there are rarely more than five qualified applicants in your pile of prospects. That's the 80/20 rule at work so use it to your advantage.

The last thing you want to do is add more to your plate by interviewing subpar candidates. Considering all combined steps of this process really involve several hours (at a minimum), why spend an entire work week interviewing when you could do it in a day and a half?

80/20 Interview questions

I have interviewed well over 1,000 workers and job candidates in my coaching career. The following steps are the result of my experience plus the application of the 80/20 rules.

Remember, if you can do the job in 30 minutes, why take two hours? I know the American culture seems to reward "paper shuffling," but if you are the leader in your business you should reward results – because that's what matters!

The steps of the interview process are simple and should be followed to the letter each and every time. The interview itself should be a 20-30 minute process maximum. If it is going longer than that it means that you, the interviewer, are doing a poor job at keeping it on task. This means that either YOU are talking too much or you are allowing the interviewee to talk too much. Either way you are wasting time and that violates 80/20 rules!

Interview Step One: Build rapport with the interviewee. This could be as simple as asking about something on their resume that you have familiarity. For example, if they play golf and you do as well then this is a natural rapport builder.(2 to 3 minutes)

Interview Step Two: Review the job description. (2 minutes)

Step Three: Ask if they have any questions about the job description. (2 to 3 minutes)

Step Four: Ask BEHAVIOR-BASED INTERVIEW QUESTIONS.

If you are not familiar with this process then get familiar with it because it is the closest thing to "predicting the future" you can hope for in an interview. These questions ask about PAST experiences with the understanding that PAST performance is the best indicator of FUTURE behavior.

Remember what I said about a worker being the best they will be in the first 90 days? Well, behavior-based questions uncover how the worker acted on day ninety one and beyond. The answers to these questions are invaluable and can save you much angst down the road.

Here are my personal Top 10 Behavior-Based Interview Questions:

1. Tell me about a time you made a mistake? How did you handle it?

2. Tell me about how you worked well under pressure.

3. Tell me about a time you had to handle a challenge? Give an example.

4. Tell me about a time you reached a goal and how you achieved it.

5. Tell me about a time you made a decision that was against the popular opinion.

6. Tell me how you set goals.

7. Tell me about a time where you had to work on a team to get something done.

8. Tell me about a time you disagreed with a coworker's decision.

9. Tell me about a time you had to motivate your team or coworkers.

10. Tell me about a time where you disobeyed a rule to get the job done.

Here are several more you can add to your arsenal:

Tell me about a time when you used logic to solve a problem.

Give an example of a goal you reached and tell me how you achieved it.

Tell me about a time when you DIDN'T reach a goal.

Tell me about a time when you had a stressful situation at work and how you handled it.

Tell me about how you worked effectively under pressure.

Tell me about a time you had to handle a challenge?

Tell me about a time where you didn't have enough work to do?

Tell me about a time you made a decision that was unpopular and how you handled implementing it.

Tell me about a time you made a risky decision? Why? How did you handle it?

Tell me about a time you had to postpone making a decision? Why?

Tell me about a time you have gone above and beyond the call of duty? If so, how?

Pick your top five to ten questions and don't worry about adding any more. If you can't uncover the past in five questions then twenty more really won't add much to it!

Once the interview is over you MUST take the time to write down any notes from the conversation. It's important you do this immediately after the interview and preferably directly on the resume or application you received. This will guarantee that you separate candidate "A" from candidate "B" in your mind. Failure to do this will guarantee that you will start blending conversations together and will have a difficult time figuring out who said what!

In conclusion, if you have done your interview well and asked the behavior-based questions you will be on your way to finding your next "all-star." Of course, there are no guarantees in new hires but you can tilt the odds in your favor by:

1. Writing a great ad.

2. Filtering resumes that fit the ad you wrote.

3. Asking behavior-based questions during the interview.

4. Taking notes during the interview and clarifying them post interview.

BONUS TIP: Conduct an interview like you purchase a new car. You would never let the car salesman know your true interest level and you shouldn't let the interviewee know either. Be courteous but impartial at all times. Keep your "poker face" on during the entire event.

Developing Workers the 80/20 Way!

Congratulations! You have chosen a new "all-star!"

The work is over, right? Wrong! The work is just beginning!

Just like your current "all-stars," the new hire is not going to walk in on Day One and be able to take over. Sure, they will walk in with POTENTIAL but you, the 80/20 Leader, must take that potential and DEVELOP them into the "all-star" you need in your business. This is how potential turns into reality!

The first step when developing workers is to train them properly on their job. And the best way to do that is to apply 80/20 principles once again!

Start with your current worker(s) who fill the function and have them create an 80/20 Activities List of their exact job function. The easiest way to do this is to have them spend two to three days writing down EVERY task of their job from the moment they arrive to the moment they leave. After two to three days the activities will start to repeat themselves and you will have your 80/20 Activities List.

With your 80/20 list in hand, it is time to begin developing the new worker. Take the Activities List and, like everything else in the world of 80/20, prioritize this list from most important to least important.

Now, look for activity groupings. For example, turning on a computer, logging into your account, and opening a program are three separate activities. But for developmental purposes they are ONE grouping because you would teach it all at one time.

When training, make sure the activity groups don't encompass more than three or four tasks at a time. Human beings do a great job of remembering in threes and fours, anything beyond that becomes harder to remember.

Don't believe me? Look at your phone number. It involves two groupings of three digits and a third grouping of four digits; and that's not by accident!

The basic training outline that can be used for ANY niche and ANY job function is as follows:

1. Start with an 80/20 Activities List.

2. Train on one activity grouping at a time.

3. Demonstrate the task to the new worker and verbalize what you are doing. (The combination of watching AND hearing the instructions will speed up the process!)

4. Have them demonstrate it back to you and verbalize what they are doing.

5. Bring in a third party, and have the new worker demonstrate the activity grouping to them.

6. If successful, move on to another activity grouping. If not, start at #3 and repeat the process.

For each training day you should plan on training NO MORE than three to four activity groupings. Remember what I said earlier about human memory? It applies here too and that is why you want to keep your training focused and in a logical order. For example, activity grouping #1 should connect with #2 and so on.

IMPORTANT: On the next day of training it is vital that you start the training day by having them demonstrate the activity groupings from the day before. If they cannot do that, retrain on their weaknesses before moving on to new training.

_In the process of developing a worker you must assure they grasp the concepts in a logical order or you risk future stumbles that could cost a great deal of money!

In review . . .

You have just spent time learning one of the most valuable exercises any leader can learn. You have discovered how to find "all-star" prospects and develop them into future "all-star" workers. You are creating the foundation for a lifetime of business success!

80/20 Organizational Principles

Organizing your business around 80/20 principles can make the difference between a "lean, mean, fighting machine" and a bloated hierarchy of non-producing team members. Remember, most businesses spend the majority of their funds on people, followed by equipment to produce whatever it is they sell.

So, with that being said, if you want to MAKE more money in LESS time then you need to assure that your #1 cost is providing the maximum value it can.

Rule #1: Make sure that a worker reports to only ONE supervisor!

The first thing you need to do is draw or print out your organizational chart. This is the chart that shows who reports to whom, who is in charge, etc.

What do you see? Do you see ONE person in charge of multiple people? If so, that's a good thing. But, quite often, you will find MORE than one person in charge of the SAME people and that is bad . . . really bad!

Having two bosses in charge of a worker is like the worker reporting to mom AND dad at the same time. Remember the dilemma of that when you were a child? You had two people looking over your shoulder and what happened? You figured out which parent was the "softie" and which was the disciplinarian – and you always appealed to the softie, didn't you?

The same thing happens if your worker reports to two people at the same time!

Rule #2: Make sure that a worker has one primary task to accomplish.

This rule is not as cut and dry because in some organizations you may have a worker who spends 50% of their work week in one area and 50% in another area but this is typically in a production type environment. When you start moving up the organizational chart to the management levels this could be a bad thing because you are becoming dependent on one worker to fill two distinct roles.

The question to ask yourself is, "If I get rid of this worker (or they leave) can I find ONE PERSON to fill BOTH of these roles?" If your answer is "yes," then you don't have a problem. If your answer is "no," you are setting up a future stumbling block. If you can't easily place an advertisement for a new worker to fill this role then you are creating a "choke point" amongst your staff and this could hinder your future growth.

Furthermore, workers should focus on one key task because that is the only way to properly exhibit the 5% of skills that make them the best at what they do. When you take a worker and bounce them around to multiple areas you will find that they are "good at many things but not great at one thing." In the world of 80/20, you want workers to be GREAT at one thing as much as possible. You want them to eat, sleep, and breathe the 5% of tasks that "all-stars" exhibit and that is how you turn a good team into a great team!

Rule #3: Apply the 80/20 to your workflow

With your organizational chart in hand, I want you to guesstimate the amount of work, by percentage, that flows through each department leader's hands.

For many, this simple task can be eye opening. Because 80/20 applies to all aspects of life you will probably find 50% or more of your work flowing through one or two leader's hands. Conversely, the remaining leaders on your team probably don't come close to handling that amount of work. Sure, they look busy (remember Pareto's Law) but they have mastered the art of paper shuffling.

On one consulting assignment I witnessed two owners with completely different working styles. Owner A was laid back but easily handled 75% of the management workload for the company. Owner B was hyper and liked to "buzz" about in a frenzy throughout the day. During worker interviews, which owner do you think the workers said was the most effective? If you said Owner A you would be wrong.

In almost 100% of the interviews they gave the credit to Owner B because he gave the perception of being overworked and dealing with many tasks at one time. But, that couldn't be further from the truth; he just voiced his "hard work" better than Owner A.

We can't forget that there are two different types of people. Some of them will work A LOT while others will work SMART. Make sure you don't reward those who just work "A LOT" without seeing the entire picture. Always take a deeper look at your team and reward the worker who is producing tangible results the quickest each and every work day. More importantly, if you are the leader of the company make sure you truly understand the difference between "working a lot" versus "smart" work. If you can't recognize the difference in yourself it will be difficult to do this with your team.

If you find this to be the case in your business, what are you going to do about it? Well, you have a couple of options and the easiest path is to consolidate the underperforming departments. This could mean the departure of a leader, of extra staff, or both. While terminating workers is painful, it will ultimately help you build that "lean, mean, fighting machine" we discussed earlier.

Rule #4: Time to change the culture . . .

Once you have made your decisions, it is time to meet with your management team and change the entire culture of your organization. Perhaps you are changing one year of poor decisions but more often you are changing decades of poor decisions that resulted in the situation you face today. Either way, it won't be easy and the only way you can get from "here to there" is to incorporate your team leaders in the process.

Before meeting with your team you must have a gut check and decide that you are really going to make these changes for the good of the business. Your managers and workers will likely resist the change at first and it is up to you, the leader, to not only show them the vision but coach them along to the finish line!

Once you lay out the vision for the leaders then you must give them their "marching orders." Tell them specifically what to say, who to say it to, and so on to spread the new 80/20 mindset throughout the organization.

Then, the most important thing you can do is reinforce the changes by having regular meetings with your team to remove any bumps in the road. Your personal involvement in the weeks and months following your announcement will make all the difference in the world.

Rule #4.1 Culture Change Continued . . .

Your next challenge is to get your managers to do the same 80/20 exercise you performed to get to this point. They should find their "all-star" 5% of workers, those who mean the most to their individual departments; the top 5% that impact 50% or more of the results.

Once you open their eyes to how this principle affects them, the buy-in will be much quicker. They will see that while they may manage dozens of workers, fewer than five workers make the biggest impact to their department.

In Review . . .

The toughest changes you and your management team will ever make involve people. But the biggest impact you will ever have on your business is by finding, managing, and building your team of "all-stars."

It's not a new piece of equipment, it's not a new client your sales team acquired; it's the men and women in the trenches that will make the biggest difference to your business's overall success.

It's my guess that doing the organizational exercise above will be the last thing on your "to do" list for a variety of reasons. But, I challenge you to change your business forever and take the first step!

80/20 Sales and Marketing

Sales and marketing are two different animals, but most people use these terms to describe the same task. That could not be further from reality! If your goal is to increase sales the 80/20 way then you MUST understand the unique differences between these two terms.

Let me explain . . .

Marketing is the art of attracting the prospect to you and your business so you can make direct contact with them and ultimately sell them your product or service.

Sales is the direct contact with a prospect who bubbled up from the marketing efforts and who is interested in buying what you produce. Said another way, it is the "feet on the street." It is the final step where you are asking for an order in some way, shape, or form.

These two terms are often misused in a variety of ways. I will often hear business owners say:

"I need to do more marketing."

What they really mean is they need to *produce more sales*. They need to make contact with a prospect who is interested in buying what they make.

All of us dream of pushing a button and having the sales roll in without any human interaction, but that is never the case. If it were, then sales would be easy and everyone would do it! But as we all know, finding and retaining new customers is one of the hardest tasks we have to do as business owners.

While the magic "sales button" does not exist, I will show you later a push-button process to keep hot sales leads rolling in day after day. For now, just know that you need both sales AND marketing to make the overall process work. There is a symbiotic relationship between the two functions and – done correctly – they make all of the difference in the world to your overall bottom line. But do one without the other and you will never reach your sales goals.

Now that we are both speaking the same language, let's move forward into the meat of the process. I promise your eyes will be opened to the simplicity of sales and how you can turn it into a "push button process" . . . with a human being attached!

The 80/20 Sales and Marketing Funnel

I have trained hundreds of salespeople and potential salespeople. At the end of the process they realize two things:

1. Sales is tough because there is not a direct "cause and effect," meaning it could be days or weeks before seeing a sale come in. This makes sales a unique psychological challenge.

2. It's not as glamorous as the movies portray it to be.

You know what I mean; the hot shot sales executive pulls up to the door in his high-priced sports car. He says a few witty phrases, closes the deal and then heads to the golf course. That's not sales, that is the Hollywood version of sales!

There is also a question that bubbles up each and every time by one or more students and that is, *"Todd, you've been doing this a long time, what's the silver bullet to increasing sales?"*

And my response each and every time is:

"The silver bullet to increasing sales is . . . doing a boring process every day."

I say this in jest to emphasize two things. First, sales is a process and it is something that every salesperson should look at as a process. It is a marathon, not a sprint. I have personally measured hundreds of salespeople as they take my instruction and apply it in the field. The salesperson who focuses on making small, steady gains on a daily basis ends up winning out over the salesperson who stops and starts throughout the year. Said another way using a baseball analogy: hitting "singles" every day is much more important than hitting the occasional "home run."

The second item I emphasize with this "boring" statement is that sales is not always glamorous. In fact, it is 95% waiting to get in front of the prospect followed by 5% excitement when they decide to buy from you. That's sales and if you don't understand this from the beginning you will probably not succeed in the long term.

If you truly want to succeed at sales you will tamp your emotions for the 95% of the time that you are doing "the process" and you won't let them get out of control on the 5% of the time you are working directly with the prospect.

Welcome to the 80/20 Emotional Scale . . .

Imagine your emotions on a scale of 1 to 10. On the scale, a "one" is the lowest of the lows emotionally. I often use the image of Eeyore from Winnie the Pooh. He is generally characterized as gloomy, pessimistic, depressed, and low energy. It's the best example of a "one" I can think of, but feel free to create your own for the purpose of this exercise.

On the other end of the spectrum is a "ten". You probably have myriad examples of this in your personal life, but for this exercise you want to picture someone (or something) that is high energy, almost to a fault. In the world of Winnie the Pooh this would be Tigger, who often enters and leaves the room with a flourish. In real life, the person who is your personal "ten" doesn't bring energy to the room; they ARE the energy in the room and, like the sun, if they are unfocused they can burn down the house!

Before we go further make sure you have concrete examples of both a ONE and a TEN.

Every long term salesperson I've worked with stays between a five and a seven on the scale at ALL TIMES. If they lose the sale they may drop to a five. If they make the sale they may rise to a seven. But they constantly stay in that zone because they realize a sale is just a sale . . . and a lost sale is just a lost sale. Neither one means more than the other if you are focused on the process!

How do you stay within that five to seven emotional range?

Get more prospect options than you can handle! This means you have more potential new customers than you realistically need to achieve your goals.

In negotiations, the person with the most options has all the power. If the buyer or seller can "take it or leave it" then they have all of the power in the room and the other party knows it. They almost smell it!

In sales, it is no different. Think about your sales career and think back to times when you had a "make it or break it" sale opportunity. Was it exhilarating? Maybe a little, but at its core it was a gut wrenching nightmare because you knew if the sale didn't go through you might run out of money, have to lay off staff, or worse, go out of business! That is a miserable place to live in the world of sales and if you plan to be selling five years from now don't let this be you!

The key to staying in the five to seven range on the 80/20 Emotional Scale is to have options, plain and simple. You want to walk in each day with three to five people you could call and one or two you SHOULD call based on the 80/20 analysis we will do later on in the book.

How does this compare to your day now? If you are like most salespeople, you walk in, spend the first thirty minutes to an hour figuring out what you are going to do today and then you start going through OLD prospects who already told you "no!" Does this sound familiar? If so, you are not alone because most salespeople were either NOT trained or were trained by people who were NOT trained. Most of the time, they were hired, given a list of leads, and given a "good luck" speech.

If this is you, don't fret. I'm going to show you a better way very soon, but before that, we have to do our homework. We must lay the foundation for a successful sales future if we expect to get consistent results from this "boring process" of sales.

It gets cold in the desert . . .

In many of my conversations with students I've trained I often have them tell me *"Todd, it's been two weeks and nothing is happening,"* or, *"Todd, you won't believe how bad my last sales call went."* There are usually specific reasons behind each of these attitudes. But, the root of the problem that is causing this attitude is the absence of 80/20 marketing.

Remember what I said earlier, sales and marketing depend on a symbiotic relationship, and while you can do one without the other, you can't make selling easy if you only choose one.

In the statements above, the real issue is that these salespeople had not instituted a good marketing plan that provided quality leads. Instead, they were relying on "old school" sales techniques.

Let me explain . . .

Going back as far as door-to-door vacuum cleaner salesmen, the typical approach to sales really hasn't changed much over the years. As a result, the turnover rate for salespeople is astronomical. What is the "old school" approach to sales? It's the famous "dialing for dollars" approach that many salespeople make as the foundation of their work day.

I am not saying that "dialing for dollars" fails to produce new sales. In fact, this common technique does work and sales *can be a numbers game*. However, this is by far the hardest and most difficult approach in the world. This is what happens when salespeople are hired by untrained and unknowing managers; they're set up from the start for frustration and failure.

Typically, 100 cold calls will get you in front of two to three people. This means if you dialed 1,000 times you would reach twenty to thirty people which is great! But, are you willing to hear 98 "no's" in the first example and 980 "no's" in the second example? Probably not, and I'm not either!

That's where the marketing part of the equation comes in. But before you can properly implement good marketing principles you must understand the "what's in it for them?" approach to understanding your customer's needs.

Let's get started . . .

Are you selling drills?

I once heard Internet marketing genius Mike Dillard tell a story that explained the "what's in it for them?" question better than anything I'd ever heard. Mike explained there is not a person alive who ever walked into a hardware store to buy a drill.

What did they want?

They wanted a hole!

Think about that for a minute. If YOU were selling drills how would you sell them? Would you describe their technological advantages in great detail? Would you talk about how cheap your drill is? Would you talk about how "cool" it looks in the customer's hands?

If you are like most salespeople you would probably start with the above specifics and may or may not go further. You would focus on FEATURES instead of BENEFITS, but remember:

Features <u>TELL</u> while Benefits <u>SELL</u>

The best way to sell the drill, or any product for that matter, is to peer inside the head of your customer and think like they would think. In the case of a drill they want a product that can produce a reliable hole in a variety of sizes at a competitive price point. Notice I didn't say "the lowest price point," because while price is important, there are other factors that go into the decision making process.

In the example of a drill, you may not want the cheapest product because it may not do the job. Maybe it doesn't have the horsepower to create the hole you desire. Or, maybe being cheaper means it will break sooner, which means you will need to buy another drill. So, when considering your own product's benefits you need to keep price out of the equation because if it is the ONLY differentiating factor between you and the competition, then you are in a weak selling position.

Let's get started with our

80/20 Benefits exercise . . .

The 80/20 Product Benefits Map

Warning (in jest): This exercise may require you to talk with customers. Since we know that 5% of your customers provide 50% or more of your sales, for the purpose of this exercise you can focus on the top 5% only.

Step One: What benefit do your customers get from your product? Write down as many things as you can think of.

Step Two: Pick the top THREE benefits. An easy way to do this is to choose the benefits that different customers say again and again. One customer's opinion is an anomaly; two or more is a trend. Respect that!

Step Three: Do customers tell you why they buy from you? If so, write down their reasons now.

Step Four: From the list in Step #3 are there two or three reasons that repeat themselves? If so, write those down now.

Step Five: How is your product different than your competition? (Focus on benefits and not features; drill vs. hole.)

Step Six: What problem do you solve? (Are you a drill salesman or a better hole salesman?)

Step Seven: What would cause your customer to start buying your product from the competition? (This should be the opposite of your benefit. In other words, if they buy because of your great service then having BAD service would be a reason they would leave.)

The 80/20 Product Benefits Map In Review

At this point you should have THREE top benefits, THREE reasons they buy from you, how your product is different than your competition, the problem you solve and why a customer would leave you. Now it's time to turn this into a benefits statement that will reshape not only your thinking, but the thinking of your entire team.

Here is a sample benefits statement. Feel free to use "as is" or change to your liking:

XYZ Company produces a unique solution to **INSERT WHAT PROBLEM YOU SOLVE**. Through our use of **FEATURE #1, FEATURE #2, FEATURE #3** we are able to provide our clients with **BENEFIT #1, BENEFIT #2, BENEFIT #3**.

Creating this statement will be one of the hardest things you will have to do. It takes time and can't be done in a few minutes. But once done it will serve as the basis for all of your marketing whether online or off.

If YOU don't take the time to peer into the minds of a customer, you are missing a valuable opportunity. Nobody knows your product's value better than your customer! They shell out the money each day, week or month to buy from you. If it wasn't valuable to them they simply wouldn't continue.

Don't skip by this exercise, or the remaining information will not have the power to change your business!

The 80/20 Sales Funnel . . . Finally!

I mentioned that sales and marketing depend on a symbiotic relationship, and this is best exhibited in the 80/20 Sales Funnel. Like any funnel, the product goes in the top and is fed out of the bottom in a specific direction. If we were talking about water, we may be funneling gushing water into a small container; something that could not happen easily without a funnel.

If we were trying to get gushing water into the top of a 2 liter bottle (with no funnel) what would happen? Well, some of it WOULD make it into the bottle but the majority of it would go just about everywhere else! It would escape, fall through the cracks and be lost forever. In sales the same thing happens if we don't have a proper sales funnel.

The entire purpose of the 80/20 Sales Funnel is to solve the problem the water funnel solves. It "grabs" a large amount of water and sends it in a specific direction. Said another way, your funnel "grabs" a large sampling of prospects and directs them into a specific direction. More specifically, it filters these prospects every step of the way until they turn into highly qualified leads. All of this is happening behind the scenes and can be going on 24 hours a day!

Your choice is simple: you can "power dial" day in and day out to a list of cold prospects, or you can spend quality time with the few prospects that your 80/20 Sales Funnel produces. Which would you rather do? Yep, me too!

A good funnel has several stages and these apply regardless of industry, product, or geography. The stages are set up in a specific order to assure you are not wasting time on weak prospects. Remember the 80/20 principles and that 5% of your prospects will produce 50% or more of the results so the 80/20 Sales Funnel is put in place to find that 5% with very little effort.

Let's get started . . .

80/20 Sales Funnel Stages

Before we proceed, let's make sure we're on the same page with our jargon. Your sales funnel should do the following:

L=P=C

Turn <u>Leads</u> into <u>Prospects,</u>

and <u>Prospects</u> into <u>Customers</u>

The first question you must answer is, *"How do you get leads?"*

The easiest way to find the answer is to do your 80/20 homework with your past customers. Do this simple exercise:

1.   How did you get your top 5% customers – the ones that provide you 50% or more of your business? Be as specific as possible.

2.   From the answers in #1, which specific advertising medium worked best?

3.   Did you stop using it? If so, what did you replace it with?

4.   Did the replacement work better? If not, what do you need to do to restart the original advertising medium immediately?

You see, the answers to your future success can be found in your present situation. But we often overlook our present successes and chalk them up as "pure luck."

Additionally, the energy we used to start these businesses is often the same energy that gets us derailed time and time again. It's okay to take a successful process and use it until it no longer works, but it is NOT okay to take a successful process and throw it out the window because a new shiny thing grabbed your attention. That is a recipe for sales death!

The point here is to pick one or two marketing methods that have proven successful in the past and DO NOT look for more until these methods have proven they no longer work. The more choices you are faced with, the more confusion that will result – and in marketing, CONSISTENTCY always wins over the "next shiny thing."

Don't believe me? Who spent $968 million on advertising last year? I'll give you a hint, it's a restaurant. More specifically, this restaurant is responsible for spending $1 out of every $6 spent on restaurant advertising in America! That means you can add up ALL restaurant advertising dollars in America and this single entity spends almost 20% of those dollars!

The answer is . . . McDonald's

I know, the amount of advertising dollars spent probably doesn't surprise you because they are a monster in this niche. But for me personally, the "why" surprises me. Doesn't it seem like every human in America *already* knows about McDonald's? Of course they do, but that doesn't stop McDonald's from continuing to spend advertising dollars. They continue to do this for one reason and one reason only; it works!

This is a great illustration on the power of FOCUSED marketing. They choose a message, choose a medium (usually print or television), keep it simple, and then they "turn on the faucet." Their television advertising catches leads at the top of the sales funnel and local billboards and print advertising sends those leads to the front door. It is one of the best examples of L=P=C and it's a very short sales cycle they repeat over and over again.

If McDonald's did not do such a great job of marketing their message, what would happen? Well, you may get a family of four coming to the restaurant and expecting a sit down steak dinner. They would be an <u>unqualified</u> prospect and they would leave the restaurant telling everyone *"They don't serve steak! Can you believe it?"*

This might be an exaggeration but it's not that far from the truth. If McDonald's didn't describe their product offering in such great detail they would have unqualified prospects lined up at their front door, who would turn out to be disappointed customers.

This same thing will happen to *your* business and *your* salespeople if you don't do a great job of turning leads into QUALIFIED prospects using the 80/20 sales funnel! You will waste many hours trying to qualify the prospect with your valuable time. In the businesses I consult for, I routinely see unqualified leads turning ten hours of work necessary to close a sale into forty hours of unproductive "paper shuffling."

A proper sales funnel can help you avoid that fate!

Create a Better Mousetrap

The first stage you must create within your sales funnel is one I like to call the "mousetrap." Like any good mousetrap, you must attract the sales leads to your funnel by tempting them with something valuable (i.e. the "cheese").

There is nothing better than valuable information; and this information should explain what the customer can do with YOUR product they can't do with your competitors'.

When we discussed buying a drill earlier in the book, I said that no one who walked into a hardware store to buy a drill really wanted a drill – they wanted a solution to a better hole!

If I were selling drills I would start by educating the customer how my drill could give them a better hole. I would explain the ease of use, the ability to create multiple holes quickly, the accuracy of the hole's dimensions, the long battery life and so on. Everything I discussed would point to making their day easier if they purchased MY drill.

When it comes to your business, your product meets a need. More importantly, it *eases a pain point* that your customer has. If it didn't then you wouldn't have them as a customer in the first place! Customers buy from you because they have a need that YOU meet better than anyone else in your niche – and that buying decision is rarely based solely on price. Sure, they don't want to spend more than necessary, but your product's solution goes much deeper than that. It's a solution to a problem, and that is the best selling proposition you can have!

Let me discuss the price issue for a minute because many of you may be hung up on the idea that "being the lowest priced product" is vital to your survival. If that is you, consider these examples:

- You can buy a watch for less than $20. Why do people buy watches for $10,000 or more?

- You can buy a used car for $5,000 or less. Why do people spend $100,000 or more for cars?

- You can meet your hunger needs for $10 per day. Why do people often spend $100 or more *on one meal?*

The point of this illustration is there are ALWAYS lower-priced products within your niche. But there are probably higher priced products too. What you must discover is the reason, other than price, your customer is buying from you. Once you discover that selling position you are ready to build your mousetrap!

Build an 80/20 Mousetrap

Step One: Review your notes from the earlier chapter and write down why your top 5% buys from you:

Step Two: From this list, find the one or two reasons that customers say again and again and write those down now:

Step Three: Take the items in Step #2 and answer this question:

My customers buy from me because:

And of the reasons above, _____ is the most important need that we meet.

It's all about needs! If you can't find one or two needs that you meet with 50% or more of your customers then you need to spend more time on this exercise because it will be the pathway to your future success.

Meeting needs IS sales.

It's not about convincing people to buy something they don't need or want. It's not about "tricking" them into buying. ***It's about taking your abilities and matching it with their needs; that's a sales call.***

The problem most of us have is we attribute our version of a salesperson to the worst sales experience we ever had. In that bad experience we were probably being sold something we didn't want in the first place! That is why we, as business people, must build sales funnels so we are only presented with those prospects who are most interested in our product.

Let's bait our trap!

Now that you have your value proposition in hand it is time to turn that into a live lead. In this situation you have two choices: an OFFLINE option or an ONLINE option, whichever meets your needs and matches your product type.

The OFFLINE option will cost more money and will probably be a longer sales cycle, but for many, this is the best approach. For example, the higher-priced your product is the more I recommend using an offline option. This is because people are less likely to buy products costing several thousand dollars over the Internet. Usually a human being must be involved in order to build trust.

The ONLINE option I recommend is email based. This means you compile some useful and relevant information and exchange that information for a lead. It also means you further qualify that lead with more email-based information until a hot prospect pops out at the bottom of the funnel.

Regardless of which option you choose, I am going to give you a basic template for each avenue. Feel free to adjust this to your needs but make sure to stick with your plan and give it time to prove itself. Do not bounce around too much between marketing tactics or you will never be sure what works!

Remember what I said earlier? *The energy that often got us INTO these businesses can be the same energy that diverts us!* Don't fall into that trap!

Offline Mousetraps

Offline mousetraps do require more money. The first thing you must do is secure a list of prospects that match the demographics of your Top 5% customer type. The more specific you can be the better. There are myriad list brokers available and they will be able to slice and dice your list to produce an exact list of leads based on the criteria you provide.

If you don't purchase your list the alternative is to hunt for leads yourself. You could call every single company in the phone book that you think is in your niche but how "80/20" is that? Not at all.

By now you should realize that we should <u>never</u> do that because our time is the most precious commodity we have. Don't be penny wise and pound foolish here. This will only cost you time – and in business, time IS money!

Before you contact your list broker you need to know the following at a minimum:

- Desired geographical location
- Company size / volume or worker count
- Years in business
- Number of locations
- Contact person's title (CEO, CFO, etc.)
- SIC code (you can search for this online)

These are the minimum requirements but there are many more items you can choose to further narrow down your list. The more specific the information you start with, the less time you will spend with bad leads; which is how we do sales in the world of 80/20!

Call your list broker or visit them online and secure a list of prospects. If you need a list broker you can find many of them on the Internet and I've provided several recommendations in the resources section of my website:

www.ToddNuckols.com/Resources

One thing to be aware of is they all use the same basic database so there is not a great deal of difference between brokers. In fact, the only main difference is if the broker QUALIFIED the lead as being real or not. Always choose this option when available. There is no use wasting your money on leads that are no longer in business!

Regardless of which broker you choose, I recommend keeping the list under 500 prospects. Your goal with the sales funnel is to find the 5% that matter. So, if you start with 500 your goal will be to find the 25 highest-potential targets. Think about that for a second, what would 25 more customers (that matched the criteria of your BEST customers) do for your sales efforts and for your bottom line? It would probably change your landscape for years to come!

With your list in hand, it is time to create the 80/20 Mousetrap. What are you offering your prospects? Is it an information-based product or is it something physical? Either one can work IF you have found this item to be highly valuable to the customer.

The first stage of your 80/20 Mousetrap involves getting the leads to "raise their hand." This means you are finding the specific lead that is interested in finding out more information about what you do. The easiest way to do this in offline 80/20 Mousetraps is to send the prospect a print advertisement that encourages them to respond.

Direct response advertising is still one of the most powerful mediums in the world because you can directly target your prospects based on any criteria you wish. With other advertising mediums like television, newspaper, or billboards it is like casting a wide net and hoping to catch something that swims by.

In contrast, direct response advertising is like using a laser to point out your perfect prospect. Either method COULD work, but we want the 80/20 method that WILL work – and in less time than ever before!

After sending your direct response piece, your process is just beginning. Most marketing gurus say that it takes *seven times* before a prospect even notices your message, but most offline marketers stop after the FIRST time! So don't stop after the first contact and make a commitment to do <u>one of the following</u>:

- Send your piece each day for at least TEN business days straight!

- Send your piece once a week for at least TEN weeks.

My preference is the first method because it will shorten the sales cycle and will draw attention to you much quicker. But, if you don't want to come across as "pushy," the second method might be a better choice.

My two cents: Feeling "pushy" is just a feeling and you really shouldn't put much merit into it. You are offering a SOLUTION to their PROBLEM. Isn't that the best thing you could ever do for another business?

With your direct response advertising it is vital that you ask the prospect to make ONE decision in order to get the valuable giveaway you are offering up. If you give them more than one option such as "Call this number OR Email us," they will often stall. In my experience, when a prospect is faced with multiple options they will often make no decision at all.

A Story About Scorpions

I live in Florida and in Florida we are often faced with a variety of creatures that lived in our neighborhoods long before the houses were built. This means you will find a few of them in your home from time to time. But I didn't grow up in Florida, which meant I was oblivious to that situation and this made me the perfect prospect for the remainder of this story.

Shortly after moving to Florida, I received a knock at my front door. When I opened it the gentlemen on the other side started the conversation by saying:

Salesperson: *"Sir, have you seen any scorpions in your house recently?"*

Me: *Scorpions??? What was this guy talking about???*

He went on to explain his real purpose of being there, which was to sell a service that protected my home from all types of creatures.

But he didn't start by saying that. He started with a message that would grab my attention immediately. He was offering a SOLUTION to a PROBLEM that virtually every homeowner had or would have.

I tell you this true story to encourage you to make your direct response advertising message a "scorpion-like message." It should grab the prospect's attention IMMEDIATELY and make them want more information immediately – as I did!

In your business, if you chose one of the direct response methods I recommend, you will have a flow of leads into your sales funnel. In just a few weeks, you successfully turned 500 prospects into 25 or more "perfect" prospects.

Your time involved was limited to getting someone to design your direct response piece and sending out 500 pieces for the daily or weekly time frame you chose. (You can even hire that process out completely which is the perfect "80/20" methodology to implement.)

Did you have to make 500 phone calls? Nope.

Did you have to be a master salesman? Nope.

Did you have to fight myriad "gatekeepers" trying to get to the prospect on the phone? Nope.

Instead, you sent direct response advertising and now you have people coming to YOU. They have "raised their hand" and it is your job to apply your solution to their problem!

80/20 Offline Mousetrap Summary:

Step One: Decide the demographics of your "perfect" customer.

Step Two: Purchase a list of prospects from any list broker you choose. Make sure that the broker has verified these leads as real and as still being in business!

Step Three: Create your direct response advertising method and choose how often you wish to send it out. I prefer a postcard or a letter but you need to stand out from the pack! If sending a letter, put something "lumpy" inside (like a golf tee) which will make your letter get opened more often.

Step Four: Give the prospect ONE "call to action" in order to get your valuable offering. Remember, the more valuable the offering is in the prospect's mind the better!

Step Five: Follow up promptly as the leads roll in. Most researchers show that if you follow up within 24 hours of getting the lead, your odds of closing the deal are several times greater!

The 80/20 Offline Mousetrap is a simple way to turn leads into prospects and prospects into customers in record time. It also removes the painful and wasteful steps of cold calling. Anyone who tells you cold calling a list of leads is the best method for reaching new prospects has been poorly trained! They probably also believe that their job is to "put in the time" when nothing could be further from the truth.

The job of the salesperson is to provide value as quickly as possible; which ultimately means turning prospects into new customers for the company. If they can do that by talking to 25 customers instead of 500 I will hire them each and every time. Bringing value beats "spending time" every day of the week!

80/20 Online Mousetraps

The 80/20 Online Mousetrap is the less expensive of the two methods, but it is also less targeted. It involves creating a mousetrap in the form of a website page that encourages the lead to exchange their information in order to receive something they value.

Don't forget that value is in the eye of the customer! What YOU think is valuable does not matter! Make sure you review your notes from the last chapter and assure you are creating a giveaway that matches the pain points of your top 5% customer list.

You need two key parts in order to do an online mousetrap:

1. A website

2. A lead capture page

Since most of you already have a website this shouldn't be an issue. However, the lead capture page is something that you obtain from the email distributor of your choice. You should NEVER send mass email from your personal email server unless you are well versed in CAN-SPAM laws. Doing it incorrectly could cost your company a great deal of money and could result in getting your website shut down altogether!

Instead, choose an email company that will allow you to broadcast emails from their servers and will take care of the ever-changing laws. I recommend several services and you can find them and more information at:

www.ToddNuckols.com/Resources

Most email service providers do a good job of allowing you to communicate in a professional way with your prospects. They will also walk you through the steps of creating your Lead Capture Page and provide you with the HTML code to insert this page on your website.

When creating a Lead Capture Page you have a few choices to make and that is based on the amount of information you want to receive from the prospect. For example, if you choose to only get their email address and first name you will get a lot of prospects to sign up, but you can guarantee they are mostly unqualified!

Remember the rules of 80/20 here and apply them to your lead capture page too. You are not focused on getting 100 unqualified leads. Instead, you are better off getting 5 or 10 highly qualified leads and spending your valuable time working directly with them.

To see an example of a Lead Capture Page in action, please check out two that I'm using at the moment:

- To give away two chapters of my book I send leads here:

    www.ToddNuckols.com/leaderbook

- To give away a FREE 80/20 Business Analysis I send them here:

    www.ToddNuckols.com/FreeAnalysis

You will notice that each page asks for a different amount of information. The first one is really "Step #1" in my sales cycle and I don't ask for as much information, but I do ask for enough to turn away weak prospects.

The second page is only available to people who have already opted in to receive my book. They are more qualified and I turn them into being HIGHLY qualified by sending them to a page where they must fill out a great deal of information to proceed.

I used to spend time calling everyone who downloaded the book. But as the number of contacts increased, I looked at the 80/20 within the 20% and now I only spend my time contacting those who fill out their information on the second lead capture page Those are the prospects most likely to want to work directly with me.

Both of the above pages are great examples of online mousetraps. They work for me because I am not reinventing the wheel. Instead I am applying principles others have taught me over the years. I encourage you to do the same because what I have shown you and what I am about to teach you are the same principles used by the most successful businesses in the world!

Getting Leads Into Your Sales Funnel

Congratulations! You now have your lead capture page set up. In exchange for your prospect's contact information, you are going to give them something of value. It could be a downloadable report or an item you send in the mail. Or, if you are selling a very high-end product, you may want to hand deliver the "giveaway" yourself. You are the judge and you should base it on the monetary value of the product you are trying to sell them.

For downloadable reports I recommend you focus on information that we discussed in the section on selling drills versus selling a better hole. You want to stress benefits of your product and how it will help the customer do something better, faster or with less expense.

For the hand delivered "giveaway" you have many more choices based on your individual product offering. I have seen salespeople deliver in depth website analysis reports to prospects, market research and search engine optimization reports. All were delivered in professional binders and some included follow up media such as a CD or DVD with more in depth information. The point here is that they gave away HIGH value information because they needed to build equity before the customer decided to purchase their HIGH dollar product.

Now the challenge is how to get people to see your lead capture page. After all, the best lead capture page in the world is still worthless if no one visits it. Thankfully, you have multiple options at this point.

You can do lead generation entirely over the Internet using Pay Per Click or PPC advertising. This is the preferred online method because you get to choose what words to target and in what parts of the country your ad will show up.

For example, if you are selling vacuum cleaners then you would place an advertisement on Google, Bing, or Yahoo that would talk about vacuum cleaners. How this works is you "bid" on search terms like "vacuum cleaners" or "buy a vacuum cleaner" and every time a person searches for that word your ad would appear. If the prospect clicks on your ad, you would be charged a fee and they would be sent to your Lead Capture Page.

The beauty of this method is you can target your prospects in multiple ways. You can choose the search terms, the time of day your ad will show, and what part of the country (or the world) it will display. Furthermore, by adjusting your bid higher or lower, you can drive more leads into your funnel and then back off if you get overwhelmed. Once you have the PPC lead generation technique set up well it is akin to turning on a faucet when you want water and turning it off when you are finished. Search marketing has been called the world's greatest marketing invention because you can get your message directly in front of people who are looking for exactly what you sell. All of this from the comfort of your office.

While PPC is a tremendous lead generation technique it is not for the timid. If you are bidding on highly competitive terms such as "golf" you will have to bid several dollars per click if you want to get your ad seen by a golf-hungry audience. Still, there are ways around that and while I don't want to get wrapped around this technique in this book, I recommend you check out this complete course on getting started with PPC:

www.ToddNuckols.com/PPC

At the link above you will find a great path for learning PPC advertising, bidding correctly, and creating the perfect online sales funnel. The learning curve on PPC is steep but the rewards are amazing and can literally change your business forever. If creating an 80/20 Online Mousetrap is the ideal path for your business, I highly recommend you put in the time to learn this method.

80/20 Online Mousetrap Summary:

Step One: Create your Lead Capture Page.

Step Two: Create your Pay Per Click campaign using search terms that describe your product best.

Step Three: Lead customers from your advertisement to your 80/20 Lead Capture Page.

Step Four: Follow up with the leads as they "raise their hand" by exchanging their personal information for your valuable giveaway.

BONUS: 80/20 Hybrid Lead Generation

If you are not ready to learn Pay Per Click advertising there is an alternative method I recommend. This method is the 80/20 Hybrid plan and combines offline advertising with an online mousetrap.

With this plan you will start with the mailing list we discussed in the offline method. Again, this is a highly targeted list of prospects that meet your "perfect customer" criteria.

With this method you will send them an offline direct response advertising piece. This piece will have the purpose of bringing them to your website to claim their "giveaway" in exchange for their contact information.

Some of you are thinking, "Why do I need their contact information? I already have their contact information!" But that's not the point. The point is to get them to say "yes" to something and when they voluntarily give up their information on the 80/20 Lead Capture Page they are saying "yes."

More importantly, they have separated themselves from the pack and have become MORE qualified, which is the entire goal of this process to begin with!

Filtering Prospects . . . The 80/20 Way!

Getting prospects is one important part of the 80/20 sales funnel but this is just the beginning. Now your real work begins!

When you turn a lead into a prospect it is no different than inviting them over for dinner. You have demonstrated a value proposition that enticed them but this is not enough. Just because you INVITED them for dinner does not mean they will come!

Why? Well, there are dozens of reasons as diverse as poor timing, other commitments, or just plain old fear of change. This is why you must take your qualified prospect and build up "relationship equity", which in business translates into trust. Trust is the one thing that will get them to "come to dinner" each and every time.

Done correctly, they will trust what you are saying. They will trust you to fulfill your promises. They will trust that they are getting value for each dollar they spend with you. They will trust you to not lead them astray. Trust is an intangible quality that ultimately translates into tangible dollars.

Think of trust like an ice cube. When building your relationship with a prospect it will take time to form that cube. But, once it is formed you can't just let it sit out on the table. You must nurture it or else it will melt. Once the ice cube melts you can't get it back. The same thing happens with trust in a business (or personal) relationship. Once the trust is gone, it's gone forever!

How Do You Build Trust?

Building trust in business is no different than building trust in your personal life. It must be done in specific stages or else it will never work. To explain this best, remember how you built a relationship with your spouse or even a good friend. Here is how it likely went:

Stage One: You built rapport by finding common ground.

Stage Two: You/They extended additional assistance in some small way which started the "trust bond." The other party reciprocated at some point.

Stage Three: Each party began to depend on the other at greater levels, continuing to build the "trust bond."

Stage Four: A new relationship is born!

Did this model align with every GOOD relationship that you have in your life? My guess is that it aligned perfectly. Sure, some of the stages probably melded together and there may not be as many clear cut spaces between steps, but it still happened.

I know this because if it DIDN'T happen you probably don't call them a friend today!

Human nature is skeptical to change, and building a new relationship in life (or in business) definitely counts as a change. Even though the new relationship could result in great value, most of us are hard-wired to view change as potential pain.

Imagine if your best friend in the world came up to you on the day you first met and said, "I want to be best friends." Or, you came up to your future spouse on your first date and said, "Let's get married." In both of these situations the receiving party would look at the other as if they were crazy.

Why should I become your best friend (or marry you)? I don't even know you! Therefore, I don't trust you to do what a best friend or spouse should do. If you don't follow through on your promises, I will be hurt emotionally.

The unspoken question is, *"What does this person really want from me?"* There is no relationship in the world, no matter how small or big, that can leap straight into a complete trust situation.

Remember back to the first time you visited the community swimming pool in your neighborhood. Remember the high dive? Was it scary? Did you run over to it, climb up and dive headfirst into the deep end? If you were like most kids, you probably didn't go straight to the high dive because of fear of the unknown.

Instead, you first decided to dive from the pool's edge. You then popped your head out of the water, realized you were still alive and were convinced you could take the next challenge. From there you may have gone to the lowest diving board and gave that one a try. Hooray! You survived!

Either the same day or your next visit you were probably ready to give the "big boy" a try. Even then you climbed the ladder with a twinge of fear because it involved climbing more steps than you were used to. Regardless, you did it, inched out to the ledge and made the leap.

This is how a personal or business relationship is built. We start at the edge of the pool and work our way up to the high dive as we build "trust equity" with the other party.

In business, the pain we foresee involves money, which means there's an even higher trust hurdle to clear. The prospect is fearful of hurting their company, hurting their image, or even hurting their job security if they are not the owner. Fear in business is all around us and if we don't confront it head-on we will turn a great prospect into "just another lead" and never get to the next stage of the sales cycle.

In business, the easiest way to build trust is by giving of yourself in a consultative capacity. If you can show prospects a better path BEFORE you ask for the sale you are building the "relationship equity" necessary to start the trust bond. The best salespeople appear to do this naturally but in reality they have learned what is important to their prospects and they have learned how to deliver that information in an educational way the prospect desires.

One word of caution here. You CAN become an "unpaid consultant" by giving away everything you know in one flurry. Make sure you are giving away information judiciously and don't fall into the trap of never thinking you can ask for the sale. After you give away some value you have earned the right to ask for something in return. Maybe they are not ready to give you all of their business at this point but if there is a "stepping stone" job you can ask for then this is the time to do that.

The 80/20 Relationship Funnel

Just like the sales funnel turned a lead into a hot prospect. The 80/20 Relationship Funnel will turn a prospect into a paying customer. But you must follow the process to the letter to guarantee the most success!

Like all things 80/20 I am going to focus on the two main areas that matter most. Yes, you could do one hundred different activities within a sales call but there are only TWO items that matter. Once you learn the intricacies of doing presentations this way, the sky is the limit.

Remember back to earlier chapters. Why do your customers ultimately buy from you and then continue to stay with you? Was it price? No, probably not. Instead, they buy from you (and stay with you) because they have a need that you meet. Said another way, they have a pain that they can't overcome without you and your solution. This is a good thing!

Ultimately, the more needs or pain points you solve for the customer, the tighter the connection gets. That's how an initial sale can turn into a lifelong customer before your very eyes.

Here are the TWO items you must do to turn a hot prospect into a paying customer. Burn this equation into your head because it will make you a LOT of money if it used correctly!

YOU + YOUR SOLUTION = NEW CUSTOMER

Does this equation make sense?

It should because it follows the four stages of relationship building I mentioned earlier. Everything starts with YOU and continues from there.

Yes, your "mousetrap" grabbed the prospect's attention but it didn't do the selling. It just caused them to pause in their tracks long enough to submit their information. Now it is up to you to make them **change direction entirely**!

It all starts with YOU.

Within the "YOU" stage, there are several subtleties that YOU will walk the prospect through. You see, a great sales call involves walking the prospect down a path YOU have created. The worst sales calls involve either not having a plan to begin with, or allowing the prospect to lead you astray – which usually gets to, *"How much is it?"* sooner than you want!

Successful salespeople all share specific traits and habits. For one, they are great listeners. They understand that in a great sales call you use the 80/20 rule once again. But this time it means you spend 20% of your time TALKING and 80% of your time LISTENING. Only by listening will you hear the prospect explain their pain. And that's a <u>great</u> thing to hear!

Before you walk in the door to talk to your prospect, it's vital that you have a plan of attack. Earlier I said that YOU are the one directing the sales call and YOU are the one who walks the prospect down the path. But none of that is possible if you don't know what path to take! Most sales calls fail before the salesperson ever hits the prospect's office door. Lack of planning will destroy your potential to close the sale each and every time.

The good news is that planning for a sales call is easy when you apply 80/20 principles. There is no need to create a different plan for every call. All you need is the 80/20 Relationship Funnel and the action you apply with every prospect you encounter. Sure, you will have to make slight adjustments along the way but that is part of the sales game. Remember, sales calls are not so much a science as they are an art. Still, when you base your art form on solid principles you increase your chances of success tenfold.

Pre-Call Question: What is the GOAL I want to achieve during this sales call?

Before you walk in the door to meet a prospect, you need a solid answer to this question. It doesn't have to be a lofty goal but it needs to be the next logical step in the relationship building process. Always think about moving the sales process forward. If you fail to do this, you will have an extremely difficult time turning a prospect into a paying customer.

Another way to look at this process is to imagine a cafeteria line with the food presented in a specific order. Typically, the first food grouping you will find is the salad, followed by the main dish, followed by the side orders, followed by dessert. This is logical because it is how the majority of human beings eat their meal.

What would happen if a restaurant had the salad, followed by dessert, with no main dish in sight? Well, a person COULD add dessert to their plate but most likely they would skip around and look for the main dish first. This would be sloppy and illogical and would clog up the decision-making process.

Make sure you are moving your sales prospect in a logical order too. Assure that you show them the "salad" first before giving them the "dessert," which in business typically involves discussing price and asking for an order.

Let's take a few minutes to develop your personal list of actions that will "move the sales process forward." Here are some examples to get you started:

- Gain a second appointment
- Identify all decision makers
- Give a tour of your facility
- Get a tour of THEIR facility
- Present a proposal of solutions
- Get an order

Only you know what the "next logical step" is within your sales cycle. Take a few minutes now and write down a few items that could be your goal when making the INITIAL sales call:

1.

2.

3.

4.

5.

Bonus Tip: The best 80/20 salespeople understand this!

Most of us have a bad idea of what the typical "salesperson" looks like. This version of a salesperson is burned into our minds because of a horrible experience being sold to at some point in our lives. For most people, this involved a "pushy" car salesman who was trying to get us to purchase a car we didn't want or couldn't afford. They seemingly couldn't take "no" for an answer and we felt uncomfortable as a result.

However, the best salespeople in the world don't act like this at all. Instead, they use the "golden rule" which means they treat others as they would like to be treated. They realize that a sales call is not about selling at all. It's about taking an emerging relationship and "moving it to the next logical step." It's about identifying needs and offering solutions that will meet those needs. The best salespeople understand this, while the underperforming salespeople don't – and probably never will.

According to statistics, it takes up to FIFTEEN other impressions to make up for one bad FIRST impression. Do you think you will get another fifteen chances with your prospect? Absolutely not! In most cases you won't get a second chance!

Making a great first impression starts with your appearance. Like it or not, people make immediate decisions about us the very instant they see us. Many times this is an unconscious decision but it will affect how they view us for the remainder of the relationship. Therefore, it is vital that you "look the part" the very second you walk in the door. It doesn't take more than ten seconds to scan yourself in the mirror, but it could be worth tens of thousands of dollars to you for years to come.

If you are unsure what "looking the part" means for your industry then pay attention to how your prospects look and dress and then dress just a bit better. For example, if your male prospects often wear a suit without a necktie you should wear a suit WITH a necktie. Dress just a little better which shows you are serious about what you are doing. If in doubt of what to wear on your visit with a new prospect, go with the highest level of dress on your personal style "scale." Always err to the more professional side of the equation!

By the way, this applies to your automobile too! You can look like a million bucks in the client's office, but if you decide to take them to lunch and they have to move around empty pop cans to sit in the passenger seat then all is lost! During a sales call you must always be "on." You can't slack off at all; especially in the beginning while you are making that very important first impression.

Finally, the best salespeople in the world realize that they are judged even after they leave the client's office. The client will now make judgments based on the promises that were made during the sales call itself. They will wait to see if you send them the email you promised. They will wait to see if you call them back on the day and time you promised. They will wait to see if you send them the product samples you promised.

The bottom line is that YOU made promises and it is up to YOU to assure delivery on each and every promise. Failure to do this will dissolve the relationship as quickly as a bad impression during your initial sales call. The worst part is that you already accomplished the hardest part of the sales call: you made a GREAT first impression and you moved them to the "next logical stage." Why would you self-sabotage by making a promise that you don't deliver on? The bottom line is to never make IDLE promises!

For example, it would be better for you to promise an email in two days (and deliver on your promise) than to tell them you will have it in their inbox in an hour and miss your deadline.

How to Develop 80/20 Listening Skills

Before we go any further in our discussion of the sales process, we need to discuss the importance of listening. It is as vital as making a good first impression, and done correctly, it can do wonders for moving the sales process forward with very little effort at all!

Have you been around people in your life who you consider to be great listeners? How about people you consider to be poor listeners? We have all experienced both, but there are surprisingly few differences that separate great listeners from bad ones.

Like everything else in life, 80/20 applies here too. There are only a few basic qualities that combine to make a person a great listener, and the good news is that this is a skill that can be learned. While you may have been "born" a great listener, my guess is you were raised in a family of great listeners. Over time, you mirrored their skill-sets without even knowing it.

Before we proceed, let's find out if you are a great or poor listener by taking this short quiz.

<u>Give yourself two points for every statement that applies to you</u>. Be honest because you need to create your personal baseline in order to improve your skills going forward.

1.   You are in a conversation with a prospect. They are talking and you stop them and interrupt. Have you done this during a sales call?

2.   A prospect is talking to you. Instead of listening you are thinking about what you are going to say next and you miss most of their conversation. Has this happened to you?

3.   A customer is talking . . . very . . . slowly. It is driving
      you crazy so instead of letting them finish, you
      interrupt and finish their sentence for them. Has this
      ever happened to you?

4.   The customer is talking. You missed something they
      said or you didn't understand a concept they
      explained. But instead of stopping them and asking
      them to repeat themselves or explain deeper you let
      them move past it. Has this ever happened to you?

5.   You are introduced to someone new. Two minutes
      later you realize you forgot their name. Has this ever
      happened to you?

If you completed this exercise honestly you can
probably recall committing several of these "listening
crimes."

   **If you scored six points or higher, YOU are a poor
listener**. But don't get discouraged! Keep reading to discover
the skill-sets all great leaders exhibit, and how you can learn
to demonstrate them as well.

80/20 Listening Skill #1:

Use Attentive Body Language

Body language is all around us and it tells more than any words ever could. It starts with a foundation of facing the person who is speaking. This one basic action can start you down a path to great success and it exhibits the most basic, but often most powerful, of all body language skills.

From here, we have to be conscious of how the most subtle body language patterns affect our chances of success. Communication is a two way process and we give and receive signals throughout the entire sales call. Most experts agree that during a conversation only 7% of the message is conveyed verbally. The corollary to this is that 93% of the message is delivered NON-verbally through our body language!

We rarely spend time analyzing the body language "signals" we give off and many of these habits are deeply ingrained in our daily life. To find out what type of signals we emit, the best way to do this is by video recording yourself while giving a presentation or mimicking a sales call with a friend or colleague.

During the taping process you must assure you are viewing all parts of your body that the prospect would see during a call. This means you need to pay special attention to your hands, arms, and facial expressions. This experiment will uncover the body language habits you exhibit on a daily basis, most of the time involuntarily. These are the way your face twitches, the way your hands move, and the constant "tics" that make you who you are.

I'm not telling you to turn into an emotionless robot. Instead, think of this as smoothing out the rough edges that distract from the real you and leave the polished diamond behind!

What are some GOOD nonverbal signals?

There are many positive body language habits we can choose from, but we all know them when we see them. Facing the speaker is probably the most important, and from there we can expand to:

- Nodding knowingly
- Keeping your arms uncrossed
- Sitting upright in your seat
- Taking notes sparingly

Be sure to look for those signals in your videotaped exercise.

What are some BAD nonverbal signals?

Examples of BAD nonverbal signals include:

- Looking around the room while the speaker is talking
- Looking at your watch
- Crossing your arms
- Putting your hand over your mouth
- Twitching in your seat
- Checking your cell phone
- Taking notes to excess and ignoring the speaker

I'm sure you have many more examples as well because these are so much easier to identify. Look for these body language "sins" and more in your videotaped exercise and make an effort to eliminate each and every one of them. Failure to do so will make your sales challenge far more difficult than it needs to be.

80/20 Listening Skill #2:
Use Your Mind Wisely

The human mind thinks 10 times faster than we speak. This means we must apply discipline when we are the receiver of information. While your prospect is talking, your mind is already looking for a way to provide an answer. This is good, and it's natural, but it can also be harmful to your active listening and ultimately to your sales chances.

The good news is your mind is working hard to come up with a powerful solution. After all, a solution to their needs is the ultimate goal. But unless we harness that power effectively we will start listening to the voices in our HEAD instead of the person sitting across the desk from us.

We've all exhibited this during a sales call, while sitting at our desk, and unfortunately even while driving a car. We literally "blank out" for a period of time while our mind spins on the topic of the moment. Or worse yet, we get lost in ANOTHER topic that has nothing to do with the conversation we are having now!

The best way to train your brain to slow down is to take notes judicially. As the prospect talks, write down one or two keywords that will trigger you later. Don't worry about writing down a full reply because that will be perceived as a bad nonverbal signal. Just a few keywords will do the trick and then you can return to intently listening to your prospect.

When it is finally your time to respond, you can use your keyword cheat sheet to demonstrate you were actually paying attention to what they said. You could respond by saying, "A moment ago you mentioned (insert keyword here) . . ." and let the conversation develop from there.

The toughest part of a sales call is handling the prospect's unspoken challenge, which is their desire for you to do two things at once. First and foremost, they want you to listen to every word they say. At the same time, they want you to retain all of their important information without looking as if your attention has been diverted.

The note-taking technique I described is the best way I know of in order to accomplish both tasks. You may need to practice doing this in order to make it feel like second nature. But once you have developed the skill, the positive responses you receive from prospects will be well worth it.

80/20 Listening Skill #3:

Control Thy Mouth!

Did you know it is physiologically impossible to talk and listen to the other person at the same time? Your mind becomes laser focused on what you are doing and it is impossible to do both.

When our minds drift during the day, we are literally hearing our brain talk to us. If we remain silent, we are "listening" and our attention hangs on every word. But as soon as we start verbalizing the words within our brain, it shuts off and instead starts listening to the words coming out of our mouth.

All of this happens in a blink of an eye but it could result in lost sales that equal tens of thousands of dollars. The 80/20 rule applies to the listening / talking equation and 80% of our time should be spent listening while 20% should be spent talking. When we talk we should address the key points our prospect brought up while they were speaking.

Become a master at this subtle sales technique and the sky is the limit!

80/20 Listening Skill #4:

Beware of Prejudice

Earlier we discussed first impressions and how they can kill a sales call before it even gets started. What you must also realize is that it occurs in reverse as well. Even before you walk in the prospect's door there is a chance you have developed a prejudice. Let me give you a few examples.

Did they write you an email? If so, how did it look? Was it well-formed or sloppy? Did they use common language or verbose sentences? Did you find any misspellings or improper grammar? These subtle cues cause you to form an opinion about the prospect before you even meet them.

Here's another example. Let's say they left you a voicemail instead of writing an email. How did they sound? Were they polite or abrupt? Did they speak clearly? Did they leave appropriate information on the message? At the end of the voicemail, did it make you happy you were going to see them soon or scared out of your mind? All of these signals shape our opinion of the prospect before we walk in the door.

Fast forward to the sales call itself.

You walk into the business, see the prospect, and shake their hand. Was it a firm handshake or a "dead fish?"

Prejudice formed!

As you walk in the office did they greet you warmly or act as if you were an intrusion on their day?

Prejudice formed!

You scan the office and find it to be busy and unkempt.

Prejudice formed!

This goes on throughout the sales call cycle and, if left unchecked, will cause you to use words and unspoken body language that ultimately reveal how you feel about the prospect. But since you're the one who's "asking for money" you must push down any prejudices and stay as neutral as possible.

You walked into the sales call with a plan to "move the process forward" and you can't let emotions get in the way. The last thing you want to do is to let the prospect's wrinkled shirt keep you from making money for years to come!

Here's one last example to think about. When was the last time you saw a man pull out a Velcro wallet? You know what I'm talking about. The one that makes that unsexy "rrrriiiippp" sound after you take it out of your pocket to pay the waiter.

If you saw a man sitting next to you pull out his Velcro wallet, what prejudice would form in your mind? That they were "uncool" or "cheap" because they didn't have a modern leather wallet? Would you instantly dismiss them as being "less than important" just from the sight of something as silly as a wallet?

The thing is, we all make these snap judgments; the challenge is to suppress those thoughts and keep an open-mind, especially on a sales call.

But back to the Velcro wallet guy. If you didn't know better, you may be sitting next to one of the richest men in the world. Who am I talking about? None other than Warren Buffet, with a net worth of roughly $60 Billion. In fact, in 2013 *Forbes* magazine reported that he made $37 million PER DAY.

What does all this have to do with the Velcro wallet? Well, in a recent television special he proudly presented his very old, Velcro wallet to the camera for all the world to see. If thirty years ago you decided not to invest with the "man who had a Velcro wallet," you would be a few million dollars poorer by now. Don't let prejudice steal your future!

80/20 Listening Skill #5:

Don't Jump to Conclusions

Because of prejudice we often jump to conclusions that can ultimately cripple our future. We make assumptions based on a dozen subtle things we may or may not even be aware of. As a result, we may not put our best foot forward in a sales call. We may not follow up on promises we made because we think, "They don't buy much of what we do anyway."

Yes, a sales call is more of a qualification event than anything else but don't disqualify a prospect without the facts in hand. Build your case first by being a great listener, asking great questions, and moving them along in the sales process.

BONUS: Quick Tips to be a Better Listener

If you don't remember anything else from this section, these three tips will help you immensely. Remember the phrase:

"Always Do This"

1.   Ask good questions

2.   Don't assume

3.   Take notes

If you just do these three things over and over again you will be thought of as one of the best listeners in the business. If you need one more example to model, think about your last doctor's visit.

While these events are not as "warm and fuzzy" as a sales call, they still exhibit the three tips above. Your doctor asks questions, doesn't make assumptions, and they take notes. Just as important, they keep a neutral face during the event (sometimes to their detriment) and they stay in control of the process.

Top Ten Listening Tips:

1. Eliminate as many external distractions as you can. Cell phones are the major issue today!

2. Eliminate as many internal distractions as you can. This means you must leave the baggage at home. Separate yourself from what happened at home or back at the office.

3. Come prepared to meetings. This means you need to have pre-determined your goal for the call. Don't forget to bring tools to take proper notes and grab an extra pen in case your first one decides to stop working!

4. Take notes judicially. This helps retain information but also keeps your mind focused and free from daydreaming.

5. Do not respond to what the speaker implies. Instead, respond to the total message. This means you must actively listen to not only the words coming out of their mouth, but their body language as they say these words. This will give you the TOTAL message.

6. Respond to a speaker non-judgmentally. Stay as neutral as possible or prejudice will creep in.

7. While taking notes, don't focus on your response at that time. Work hard to stay focused on the speaker as you take "keyword" notes that will help you formulate your response at the appropriate time.

8. Do not go into a situation with your mind already made up. As we spoke of already, prejudice can keep us from gaining tens of thousands of dollars over the life of a customer. Don't let that happen to you!

9.   If you find yourself not listening, physically move forward in your seat an inch or two, or lean towards the speaker. Either physical movement will cause your brain to respond by focusing on the speaker.

10.   Finally, even if you are doing a team sales call, don't rely on your teammate to take all the notes. In fact, BOTH of you should take notes and compare facts afterwards. It's amazing how multiple people can hear the same information and interpret it differently!

This lesson on listening skills may become the most valuable skill-set you ever learn and develop. It will cause you to gain respect from prospects because rarely do they get listened to in an appropriate manner. You will stand out from the pack (in a good way) and that is the best thing that could ever happen in a selling situation!

Selling "YOU" the 80/20 Way

Like any personal relationship you are trying to build, a selling relationship will follow the same basic steps. These steps are built upon human nature and must be adhered to or failure is almost guaranteed.

To begin with, all long-term relationships begin with one thing and one thing only – rapport. Think about it for a minute: on a golf course or at a party you are introduced to someone and what is the first thing you say after being introduced? If you are like most people you ask, *"What do you do?"* This is done instinctually but its one basic purpose is to develop rapport.

Creating rapport has the purpose of establishing common ground. When you create a commonality with another person you increase the comfort level and grow the relationship from this basic foundation. Think of it as building a house; you can't put on the roof without the walls, and you can't put up the walls without the foundation. Relationships are no different.

From a selling standpoint, the easiest way to build rapport is to be observant. Quite often we walk into a sales call with blinders on. We have our goal set in our minds and no matter what we are going to get there! But, we can't forget that sales relationships involve two or more human beings connecting and it is not simply a matter of "checking the boxes" and moving on. It's about reading the total message (i.e. body language) and responding in kind.

As you walk through your prospect's front door, begin to scan the room for obvious points upon which you can build a new relationship. Look for awards on the wall, trophies on the shelf. Once you enter their office you are in their personal space and the scanning should continue. Is there a golf or bowling trophy on the shelf? Pictures of a son or daughter in a military or little league uniform?

Be observant and actively look for points of connection. Like the ability to uncover needs, the more "rapport building" connection points you can find the stronger the foundation will become.

Take time to build rapport and the rest of the relationship building process becomes much easier. Break this rule and you will be fighting an uphill battle forever!

Uncover needs the 80/20 Way!

With a solid foundation of rapport established, it's time to move to the real purpose of your sales call which is to uncover needs you can meet. Remember, a sales call is nothing more than matching a customer's needs with your abilities. It's not an "arm twisting" event but simply a solution to their problem!

Because a great 80/20 sales call involves LISTENING 80% of the time and TALKING only 20% of the time it's important that you make your words count. In order to do this you must ask appropriate questions that will ultimately get the prospect talking about their most pressing needs.

There are three basic types of questions and all three should be used at the appropriate time in the conversation. The three question types are:

Open-Ended Questions: These type of questions are the who, what, when, where, and how questions. The sole purpose of this line of questions is to get the prospect talking. These questions will have unlimited response choices but that's okay.

Think of these questions as "casting the net" to see what you pick up out of the ocean. Yes, you may get a few bits of debris (i.e. unnecessary conversation) but you may also catch a few fish (i.e. prospect's needs).

Closed-Ended Questions: This second type of question is a more narrowly focused question that requires a more specific answer. These types of questions should only be asked when you have uncovered more information from the prospect through the open-ended question types.

For example, if you find out that delivery times are an important need for the prospect, you may follow up with a closed-ended question such as, *"If you don't get your product delivered to the warehouse on time, how does that affect you?"*

Yes/No Questions: As the category suggests, there are primarily two responses you can get to this kind of question: "yes" or "no." This would be the final question you would ask a prospect to drive home a point. It works beautifully when you have uncovered an important need.

Sticking with the delivery time need we uncovered in the example above, you would follow up the Closed-Ended Question by saying, *"If I understand this correctly, on time deliveries to your warehouse are vital to your supply chain. Is that correct?"*

In review . . .

If you started your conversation with Open-Ended Questions and found out that delivery times are crucial to the prospect you would have uncovered a need. Next, you would have asked a Closed-Ended Question to get the prospect to focus on how important that need really is. Finally, you would end that line of questions with a Yes/No Question to drive home your point. By the way, it's okay to magnify a need IF you do it in the way I've described above and especially if you have a solution for that need. In fact, it's vital for success!

Think of these question types as the key to getting your prospect to walk down the sales path YOU have chosen. Done correctly, they begin the conversation, realign the conversation if you get off track, and finally bring the conversation to a successful close.

BONUS: Scared, Uncertain and Doubtful

Every prospect you speak with is a bit scared, uncertain, and doubtful about choosing your company to handle their needs. This is basic human nature and you can use it to your advantage!

In the example above, we used "delivery times" as the uncovered need that was important to the prospect. We then focused on that "delivery time" issue by saying, *"If I understand this correctly, on time deliveries to your warehouse are vital to your supply chain. Is that correct?"* This was done for the primary purpose of reminding the prospect of a BIGGER fear than changing over to your company's solution.

Not all fears are created equally and the fears that affect them personally (like job loss) are the ones that will sit at the top of their list. In comparison, working with you versus another vendor is not a great fear; it's the RESULTS that occur from working with you versus another vendor that they are scared of. You can position yourself as a person who would NEVER let that pain happen to them. Done correctly, you will go from being just another salesperson to becoming their security blanket in a blink of an eye.

80/20 Selling Wedge

To make the questioning process easier to remember, I've developed a visual aid to assist you. This is something I've taught hundreds of students over the years and until I introduced "the wedge," they were prone to asking questions in an illogical order.

This is the 80/20 Selling Wedge:

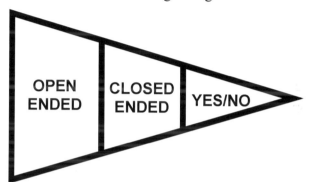

Like the three types of questions we discussed, "the wedge" is designed to work from left to right. This means the broadest part of the wedge will trigger you to ask the broadest question types. The next stage becomes more narrow and it reminds you to ask more narrow questions. Finally, the tip of the wedge is the most focused and it reminds you to ask questions that result in the most focused answers.

If you remember nothing else, burn this image in your head and during a sales call move from left to right and you will increase your chances of success exponentially.

Still, there are specific hurdles you have to cross at each state of the **80/20 Selling Wedge.** Let's begin . . .

Open-Ended Questions

There are several goals you hope to achieve at this stage of the sales call. Both parties are brimming with questions; there is information YOU want to find out about the prospect and THEY have questions they hope to get answered by you. And the quicker they can get an answer the better!

The first question you must address is the prospect's unspoken thought:

Who are you?

Remember, your prospect probably gets pelted with dozens of sales calls per week. To them, you are just another "sales face" in the crowd. It is vital you get your message across clearly and quickly. You already have an advantage because they responded to one of your advertising methods, which means they at least have "some" interest in hearing about you and your business. But that's not an invitation to waste their time! There is nothing more important to a busy prospect than respect of their time!

The worst thing you can do is not prepare to explain WHO you are. If you are planning to just respond "off the cuff" you are guaranteed to flub it nine times out of ten. The best salespeople are ALWAYS prepared for the call and planning your introductory script is the best way to do it.

By the way, scripts are NOT bad. The problem we have is our experience with scripts typically involves BAD scripts that are used on us. How many times have your received a telemarketer's call that involved a bad script? Probably too many times to count.

The reason this script stood out as being weak and unprofessional is because it was:

1. A bad script.

2. Not practiced sufficiently.

3.   Not written the way we naturally speak.

All of us write and speak completely differently. We tend to speak in short, choppy sentences and we write in fuller, more verbose sentences. If you don't write a script that fits the way you talk you will sound like a telemarketer each and every time!

In addition, it's important to note that we have all experienced GREAT scripts and didn't even realize it. When was the last time you saw a movie or television show? Guess what, they were using scripts! But they were using well-written scripts that were constructed in the way we all naturally speak. It's not that scripts in general are bad; it's that poorly assembled scripts are the culprit. Don't make that mistake!

In order to explain "who you are" in a timely and efficient manner you need to first write down what you want to say. Give it a try now:

WHO YOU ARE:

Now, take a look at your script and cross out any unnecessary words. Your goal is to remove at least half the words from your written script. When you do this you are converting your message into a form that matches the way you speak, which is the goal. Give it a try for the next few minutes.

WRITE OUT YOUR NEW SCRIPT:

Do you see a difference between the first script and the second one? If done correctly you should see a marked difference between the two. Now, put this exercise to the side and come back to it in a few hours. By stepping away from the task for a bit, you'll be able to tackle it with a fresh perspective later. If you are like most of my students, you will find that a third review will result in even more words being removed.

The final stage of this, and all script creation, is to record yourself saying the script. Assure that it sounds natural and is in the language you would normally use if you met a friend on the street. The more natural you make your script the more professional you will sound. Plus, you have a better chance of memorizing it when it is in YOUR language instead of the jargon of another person.

Now that the prospect knows "who you are," it's time to answer their next question:

Why are you here?

Done correctly, this question is answered in conjunction with your introduction. If you followed the lead generation techniques I discussed earlier, your prospect will already have the answer to this question (but it's okay to remind them). By telling them a specific reason for your visit, it comforts their minds and they won't assume you are going to ramble on like many salespeople are prone to do.

Like the *"who are you?"* question, I recommend you script out and practice your *"why are you here?"* answer as well. ***Poor preparation equals poor delivery, which translates into lost sales*** more times than not. Don't let that be you!

If you managed to get through the first two steps of the conversation then congratulations! You have begun the conversation on a positive note which means you've earned another few minutes of the prospect's time. While you can't drop your guard just yet, you can dig deeper with your line of questioning. Your goal at this point is to uncover two additional layers of foundational conversation that will strengthen rapport and begin uncovering the prospect's needs.

Now is the time to use the first part of the **80/20 Selling Wedge** which involves Open-Ended Questions. While you can ask anything you wish, I recommend you follow the plan I am about to outline. This is something I have personally tested in the field and it works. As you make more sales calls you may find nuances that work better for your situation – and by all means, use them!

Open-Ended Questions:

Connecting with prospects on a personal level

If you go into a conversation with a stranger you will typically walk out of it thinking they are either:

A.)   The greatest person on earth

B.)   A jerk

Now here's the beauty of this: there is ONE primary reason that separates the "A" person from the "B" person. What is it? Want to take a guess? Go ahead, I'll give you a minute . . . tick, tick, tick . . . .

Okay, here it is . . . the primary difference between person "A" and person "B" has nothing to do with their looks, physical size or shape, or even their bank account. The key difference is that person "A" asked about YOU. Simple as that.

They asked how you were, what you did, how long you have done it, what did you do before, and so on. When you spend time talking about YOU the person sitting across from you looks like a hero each and every time.

Knowing this, it's important for you to get the prospect talking about themselves as soon as your introductory script is over. Again, the way this is done is by asking the right questions in the correct order!

Prospect's PERSONAL Questions

Okay, you have introduced yourself and explained why you are there. Now you need to throw the ball back in their court and give them the stage to talk about themselves. You should begin this by asking questions that show you care about them as a person. The rules of human nature state that the #1 person in your life is YOU. Use this fact to your advantage during a sales call by selflessly asking questions that get the prospect talking about themselves.

While you can ask myriad "personal" questions here are a few of my favorites in the order I recommend you ask them.

1. Mr./Ms. Smith, what is your primary role with the company?

2. How long have you been in this position?

3. What role did you have prior to your current role?

These three simple questions will get the prospect talking about the most important thing in their life . . . THEM! From here, you need to naturally go into the next stage of rapport-building questions and ask them about their company.

Prospect's COMPANY Questions

Once you reach this stage you are cooking with gas. They liked your introduction and they've just spent the last several minutes talking about themselves. It is a perfect time to lead them further down the path. This time you want to crack open the vault a bit more and find out more about their company.

Once you take the step into the realm of "company questions" you are guaranteed to start uncovering needs. One word of caution though: it is much easier to ask important questions if you have done your homework. In today's world your homework involves checking out their website and searching online for any recent news stories involving their company.

Assuming you know the background of the company, see if you can find out the following:

1. How long have you been at this location?

2. Where were you previously located?

3. Do you have other locations or satellite offices?

4. (If applicable) How do these other locations fit into your overall process?

5. Who are your customers?

    OR

6. Describe your ideal customer type.

We don't want to go much deeper than this line of questioning at this point. Remember, every stage of a relationship (personal or professional) involves a delicate dance of giving and receiving. If the prospect feels they are "giving up the goods" too quickly, they are likely to clam up at this point, so be cautious. Be an <u>active listener</u> and show empathy; don't be a robot!

The questions we have asked at this point all fall in the widest section of the **80/20 Selling Wedge** which means they will return the widest possible gamut of answers, but that's okay! This is why it is vital to use your newly-honed listening skills so you can key in on any small nugget they dispense. These nuggets should ultimately uncover needs and as you know, needs are the gold you're digging for! The more needs you uncover, the better your chances of being able to solve those needs with your product or service.

Closed-Ended Questions:

Establishing Your Position

With needs uncovered it is time to move down the sales "path" and bring the prospect closer to becoming a customer. Your work is not done but you have made great strides so far– congratulations!

The way we move them forward from this point on is by asking more specific closed-ended questions. Remember, these are questions that require more specific responses. Like a good lawyer, we should NEVER ask these questions unless we are certain of the answer we are about to receive. We are asking them in order to achieve the following purpose:

We remind the prospect of their important needs AND we demonstrate that we were listening!

Ultimately, the closed-ended questions we ask will establish:

- <u>OUR</u> strategic position in the sales call "relationship." This is vital because if we are just wasting our time with a conversation that is going nowhere, we need to find out sooner rather than later!

- The <u>PROSPECT'S</u> position in regards to what they are trying to accomplish. Are they really looking to make a change in their company or are they looking for a free lunch from another salesperson? The worst thing we can do is waste our time with a prospect that has a completely different objective than us. By the way, it's okay to "fire" a prospect if your desires and their desires do not align!

What is <u>YOUR</u> position?

When establishing your position within the sales call "relationship" you should work to uncover two key areas:

1. Who is your competition?

I'm sure you know the companies you compete with in general, but you must find out who you are competing with <u>specifically</u> in this situation. Finding this out can be one of the most valuable pieces of information you ever find because every competing company within your niche has a reputation, good or bad, and you can use this to your advantage.

As soon as you establish your chief competitor you know several key things immediately:

- They are bigger than you
- Or, they are smaller than you
- They have more capabilities
- Or, they have fewer capabilities
- They have a great reputation in the market
- Or, they have a poor reputation in the market
- They are the MOST expensive
- Or, they are the LEAST expensive

Do you see how powerful this information can be? It is like going into a boxing match and already knowing your opponent's strengths and weaknesses. Knowing where the "punch" is going to come from allows you to create a plan to avoid it entirely.

What if they are <u>BIGGER</u>?

Most people assume that if their competition is bigger they will always win. But don't forget that Goliath went down in the battle! Bigger doesn't always mean better, and it can often mean:

- Lazier
- More complex structure
- Less attention to customer needs
- Less likely to adapt to market changes
- Less personal attention to customers

The list can go on but you get the point. Bigger <u>can be</u> better, but it is <u>not always</u> better.

If you find yourself competing with a bigger company, it's important to expose your advantages as the <u>smaller</u> company. You should show the prospect that:

- You are more flexible.

- The prospect is NOT just another "sale."

- You can adapt to constant market changes.

- You don't have the expensive overhead of your competition.

- You are dealing with ME, the owner (if applicable).

Now let's flip the tables and assume you are the BIGGER company who competes with the SMALLER company your prospect currently buys from. In this case you must position yourself as:

- A market leader.

- A company that has strength in numbers.

- A company that has backup machinery / systems in place to remove the fear of something breaking.

- Having MANY professionals to meet your needs instead of one or two.

- Demonstrating longevity (if applicable).

The point of this exercise is that it doesn't really matter if you are the biggest or smallest in your market niche. The most important things you can do are:

A.) Find out <u>your position</u> and

B.) Use it to your advantage to strengthen your stance in the sales call.

80/20 Competition Exercise

Step One: List three to five of your direct competitors:

Step Two: Which ones are BIGGER than you?

Step Three: Which ones are SMALLER than you?

Step Four: Write your response (to the prospect) when faced with one of the BIGGER competitors:

Step Five: Write your response (to the prospect) when faced with one of the SMALLER competitors:

What is <u>YOUR PROSPECT'S</u> position?

Now that you know where you stand in the sales call "battle" relative to your competition, it's vital to find out where your prospect stands. Remember, they have a lot on the line too. They are deciding whether or not to change from a proven vendor (in most cases) to your company. Even if you offer a better solution you are still a "change" and human nature always resists change!

2. *How does the prospect "win" the sales call?*

In every sales call, each party has an objective they are trying to achieve. For you, the objective is easy because you are trying to move them down the path from being a prospect to a new customer. That is your primary goal and every action you take heads toward that moment. Similarly, the prospect has his or her own agenda. If the two of you are to come to an agreement, you need to find out how the prospect "wins" as quickly as possible.

If you've made more than a handful of face-to-face sales calls, you understand that the prospect's goal and your goal don't always align. This is a state of nature in the world of selling and the only thing you can do is find this out as early in the process as possible so you don't waste your time.

Remember, you have a handful of filtered and highly qualified prospects at your disposal. Your sales funnel vetted them for you! The worst thing you can do is discontinue the proven sales funnel vetting process because you feel desperate or anxious. YOU have customer options and in negotiations, the person with the most options has the most power.

Finding out how the buyer "wins," even if it disagrees with your goal, is not necessarily a deal killer. It is simply another uncovered need and you can decide how you want to meet that need. You can create solutions (if it fits your overall goals) or you can walk away from the deal entirely (if THAT fits your overall goals). Yes, you want a new customer but not at the expense of crippling your business!

It is important to understand that buyer's "win" in many different ways. For some, esteem in the eyes of their boss is enough to justify a "win." For others, cost savings or increased productivity is their goal. Finding out what drives the prospect to make a change is vital to tailoring the conversation to meet his or her needs.

There are many questions you can ask a prospect at this point of the sales call but here are my personal favorites:

- If you had a magic wand and could fix one item about your current vendor, what would you change?

- How soon are you looking to make a decision about this project?

- Is a change in vendors based on budgetary reasons? (*This is a key question because it will show you if being the "lowest priced vendor" is most important to them.*)

I recommend you take time and develop questions that YOU are comfortable saying. Whatever you ultimately decide to ask, just make sure you are filtering out the prospect's needs to assure they properly align with your capabilities.

Yes/No Questions:

Magnify the <u>value proposition</u>!

If you have made it this far in the sales call you have completed several important filtering stages. You have:

- Built a foundation of rapport.

- Uncovered needs.

- Narrowed those needs to a few important ones.

- Discovered your position versus the current vendor or other competitor.

- Discovered how the buyer "wins" by choosing you.

- Decided the buyer has needs you are willing to meet in order to achieve your overall goals.

To the prospect, you have done nothing more than have a conversation. But if you were to videotape the conversation you could literally check off those bullet points one by one. Done correctly, you "checked the boxes" in the proper order because the sequence of the conversation is vital. If you violated the rules, your prospect probably feels a little off-kilter and unsure of your true intentions. You can't violate human nature! But if you did it correctly they now view you as an ally in the process. Great job!

To wrap up this stage of the process you need to magnify the expressed needs to cement your position. Don't assume the buyer will remember their needs; it's up to you to do it for them!

The easiest way to do this is by reviewing your keyword notes and look for the top one or two needs they expressed. From there, use the following script:

Start Your Script With:

"As you mentioned earlier . . ."

OR

"I remember you saying . . ."

End Your Script With:

*"How would (**NOT MEETING THAT NEED**) affect you?"*

OR

*"What impact would (**NOT MEETING THAT NEED**) have on your company?"*

This ending script has the opportunity to win the sale for you quicker than anything you have said thus far. It is the crescendo to a great movie that is playing out. Your prospect is now left with the thought that:

A.)   They DO have an important need that is unmet.

B.)   If this need continues to be unmet it could spell out gloom and doom for the prospect and his or her company.

Fear is a powerful motivator and used correctly CAN get a prospect to change from their current vendor to you, but only if you have properly set up the sales call process according to the rules we have discussed.

A sales call is a dance. Up to this point all you have done is convince them to dance with you. You really haven't got them to the dance floor just yet, but you are close. In the next chapter we will talk about presenting your solution (i.e. getting them on the dance floor) and getting them to say "yes."

Presenting Your Solution

If you followed the steps correctly, you uncovered one or more of the prospect's most pressing needs. Only then can you present your solution to the prospect.

Failure to uncover needs followed by "presenting your solution" means you will offer the prospect generic solutions which may or may not apply to them. You can talk about how you have met needs in general but you can't give them a specific solution to a specific need and that puts you in a much weaker position.

Presenting a handful of generic solutions is like throwing spaghetti noodles on the wall to see what sticks. We've all experienced it in our business lives, probably as both the culprit and the victim.

One experience I had was as a casual observer at an office supply store. I was shopping for products and was approached by two salespeople who had just walked in to offer their wares. The problem was, I happened to be wearing a shirt that was the <u>same color</u> as the executives at the office supply store. So, they assumed I worked there and walked over to begin selling me their SOLUTIONS.

For a full minute or two, and without asking my name or qualifications, they began to spout off the various features they could offer "my" company. After letting them continue (so I could have this story to tell) I told them I didn't work there and pointed them in the direction of a worker. I watched them do a beeline directly to the worker and, you guessed it, go straight back into their "solutions" script.

While this is a hilarious and extreme example, it was very real. In fact, I'm sure it happens far more than it should because most salespeople <u>do not have customer options,</u>

which means they walk into every call as a desperate and scared human being. This drives their actions and they do anything they can to "get to the sale." Unfortunately, this has the exact opposite effect on the prospect than the one they intended. The more the salesperson pushes, the more the prospects resist.

Why are you different?

When it is time to present your solution, it is vital for you to show the prospect that not only is <u>your solution</u> different but that <u>YOU</u> are different as well. If you are unable to show a true difference in their current vendor versus you then why should they change at all? <u>Differentiation</u> is the key ingredient to overcoming the dreaded "commodity" tag.

If all vendors within your niche are viewed the same then it generally comes down to price as the differentiating factor. A low price (if applicable) should be a side benefit of doing business with you and not the primary benefit. If customers only buy from you because you are the lowest price in town then the relationship is weak. It also means they will leave you when someone else offers your "commodity" product for a penny cheaper.

We discussed differentiation when we talked about competitors who are bigger or smaller than you. This is great, but it's just a start. True differentiation goes much deeper and paints the entire picture for the prospect. You should walk away from the sales call with the prospect left thinking:

"I must do business with this company or I risk future pain. They bring something to the table I've never seen before."

If you can walk away from every sales call with this thought in the prospect's head then you are on the right track to proper differentiation. In classes I've taught, I find it to be easier to break your differentiation into segments. Once this exercise is complete, you can group it all together as a powerful statement that grabs the prospect's attention.

Answer the following questions:

1. We are different than (COMPETITOR NAME) because . . .

Answer this question for every direct competitor you find in your market. In most cases that will only be three to five others because the 80/20 rule applies here too. I would not bother to go past five direct competitors because it will give you diminishing returns and waste your precious time.

2. We have a reputation for . . .

Believe it or not, every company has a reputation in their marketplace. I know this because I've asked thousands of workers this question and they have all answered it. Typical responses are:

- *We are the cheapest price in town.*

- *We are the most expensive shop in town.*

- *We are the most professional in our niche.*

- *We are always on time with our promises (or we aren't).*

Every business has a reputation in their market and yours does too. If you are unsure what yours is, ask your workers – they will tell you!

3. My company is successful within my niche because . . .

If you've been around for more than a year, you must be doing something right. You have figured out how to solve a problem in a way others have not. Dig deep and write down why you are successful. Then ask your workers to do the same thing and compare notes. By involving different parties in this exercise, you are more likely to find out the true worth of your business.

If you have finished answering the three questions above, it's time to create your differentiation-based solution statement. There are two forms you need to create and the second version should expand on the first.

Version #1 is called the ***80/20 Solution Statement.*** Just like all things 80/20, you should get out the most <u>valuable</u> information in the <u>shortest</u> time period possible.

Your goal should be to demonstrate **80%** of your <u>most valuable differentiations</u> in **20** seconds or less. This is NOT about telling your entire company story. It is the billboard on a busy interstate that grabs a driver's attention as they speed by at 70 miles per hour.

If you are sitting in a sales call and have reached this stage you need to present a solution to the prospect's needs while weaving in your company's differentiations. It's not just about meeting needs; it's about meeting needs in a unique way that will make you stand out from your competition in the best way possible!

<u>BONUS:</u> The ***80/20 Solution Statement*** can also be used when you meet a complete stranger at a business event and they ask, *"What do you do?"* Obviously you do not have the advantage of knowing what is important to them, so you must assure your ***80/20 Solution Statement*** is the billboard on the interstate that makes them say, *"Tell me more!"*

This response is your ultimate goal after delivering your solution statement. You WANT the prospect to ask for more information because you tickled something in their head they are missing from their current vendor.

If you have just delivered the perfect solution statement and are faced with the *"Tell me more"* response, how do you respond? Well, a poorly trained salesperson would destroy their opportunity by spouting off feature after feature to see what sticks to the wall. But a seasoned **80/20 Salesperson** would respond quite differently.

An **80/20 Salesperson** will hear the *"Tell me more"* question and immediately revert back to the early stages of a typical sales call. They will IMMEDIATELY begin asking **Open-Ended Questions** that have the sole purpose of getting the prospect talking. What happens after that? Well, we know that these types of questions get the prospect to discuss their needs. Once we hear a need, we know we've struck gold once again! Walk the prospect down the path, and turn them into a customer if they are a good fit for YOUR needs.

Closing the Deal the 80/20 Way!

You have made it through 90% of the sales call but you aren't done yet. Depending upon the product being offered, the previous stages may have occurred in one meeting or a series of meetings. Maybe you can open and close the same day or maybe you have to work over a period of weeks. The bottom line is that the job is not done yet; finish strong!

You will know you are ready to "close the deal" when you start to hear buying signals from the prospect. These can come in many different forms, but hold off on directly responding to their question and immediately going into your "closing the deal" script.

Examples of buying signals are:

- *How much is your solution going to cost?*

- *When can we expect delivery?*

- *When do we have to make our decision?*

- *How soon can we get started?*

- *What do you need from us to get started?*

When you hear questions like this your adrenaline should start to pump because you have done your job to perfection. But don't let that emotion overpower the remaining parts of your sales call process. Remember, stay between a FIVE and a SEVEN on the emotional scale because YOU have all the options!

Like all parts of the sales process, asking for the order should be a well-rehearsed script. Remember, it should be in your own language and it should be practiced to perfection. By no means should it come "off the cuff" or you risk ruining all of your hard work.

The process I prefer works with any buying signal they present to you. This process should preferably be used immediately after the buying signal question but can be used without it as well.

Step One: Review their needs with the following phrase:

> *"Mr. Smith, you mentioned that (THEIR NEED) was most important to you. We can meet that need by (INSERT UNIQUE SOLUTION)."*

Step Two: Present the price and ASK for the order.

> *"We can take care of everything for $X,XXX (or quote a PER PIECE price if applicable).*
>
> *Are you ready to get started?"*

If you are like most salespeople a tingle went down your spine when you thought about quoting a price and asking for the order. After all, there is no going back at this point. There is no more soft-selling that can be done. You have only one thing left to hear: a "Yes" or a "No."

If they say "Yes," your work is done. Proceed to the next steps of your process, collect the necessary information and schedule a FOLLOW UP EVENT. It is vital to get the prospect thinking about the NEXT EVENT instead of the decision they have just made.

If you get them too focused on the fact they are changing from a proven vendor to a new vendor they are liable to suffer from buyer's remorse. Fear of making the wrong decision and fear of losing their job will creep in. This means all of your hard work can be thrown out the window <u>even if</u> your solution is better!

This next event needs to be soon and should be the same business week if possible. It should also be an event that starts the process of changing to your solution. You should get them to give you the specs of the job, fill out a credit application, or provide you the information necessary to get started. Whatever the next step is, just make sure it is SOONER rather than LATER and ensure it starts the buying process!

What if they say "NO"?

If they didn't say yes then obviously they said "no." However, as an **80/20 salesperson**, you know that not all "no's" are created equal. In fact, they mean two completely different things if you are trained to spot them.

When the prospect gives you a negative response about preceding it will come in one of two forms. It will be a:

STALL

or

OBJECTION

The reason you must identify which negative response you received is so you can apply the appropriate strategy. The sales call is not dead yet if you have practiced your *stall* or *objection* scripts.

Stalls

Stalls are the easiest form of objection to overcome. An example of a stall would be:

- *"Call me tomorrow."*

- *"Let me think about it."*

- *"I'm not sure just yet."*

- *"I don't know; let me get back with you on this."*

When a customer delivers a stall, their unspoken thoughts are:

"I do not have a specific reason for hesitating . . . I'm just not sold yet; sell me more!"

Stalls are <u>vague</u> responses to specific questions. You asked, "Are you ready to proceed?" and they said, "I'm not sure." If they weren't stalling they would have said, "Yes, let's get started," or "No (followed by a SPECIFIC REASON)."

If you are faced with an ambiguous response to a precise question, it is time to implement your ***80/20 Stall Strategy***.

Step One: Start with *"I understand how you feel . . ."*

Step Two: *"Earlier you said that [INSERT NEED(s)] was/were important to you."*

Step Three: *"If these [SPECIFIC NEED(S)] were not addressed, how would it affect your business?"* (let them respond)

Step Four: After they respond you will then say, *"Because these needs are important, we don't want those (preferably disastrous) things to occur. This is why we will [REMIND*

THEM OF YOUR UNIQUE SOLUTION] to ensure this never happens to you."

Step Five: ASK for the order again.

This approach does a few key things, all built on the human need to avoid pain at all costs. You are first and foremost sympathizing with them. This is important because they are so used to salespeople talking "down" to them at this point. They often make the prospect feel inferior or stupid for not buying their product or making up their mind in a timely fashion. These of course are poorly trained salespeople that let their desperation and adrenaline get the best of them.

Second, you are reminding them of needs they expressed during the sales call. If you don't remind them of the potential pain, their brain will push it down deep inside their cortex and it won't show its ugly head again until it actually happens with their current vendor.

Once you have "humanized" yourself and also reminded them of their important needs, then you are presenting your solution once again. It's not that your prospect doesn't want a better vendor solution. There are obviously issues with their current vendor or they wouldn't have called you into their office in the first place.

The problem lies in the overworked nature of today's workforce. The prospect you are talking to is probably doing the job of two or more workers due to corporate downsizing. The prospect would love nothing more than to take something OFF their plates and hand it to a trusted vendor. But due to fear of it backfiring on them, they are cautious to proceed.

This is why you have to present a unique and confident solution to the situation. In fact, if you can weave in statistics or how you've helped others in similar situations, all the better. They *want* to give you some of their workload so let that fact give you the confidence you need to ask for the order again, which is the final step of the *80/20 Stall Strategy*.

Human beings do not typically want to be mean-natured. Because of this, most of the negative responses you get will be stalls and you must be prepared to use this strategy several times if necessary.

Objections

When you asked for the order the first time, you probably received a stall. If after using your *80/20 Stall Strategy* you get another negative response, this time it will most likely be an objection.

Objections, unlike stalls, are SPECIFIC reasons for not wanting to do business with you. You will know these when you hear them because if you have sold for more than two days you have heard them already, I'm sure of it.

Here are a few examples of objections:

- *"Your price is too high!"*

- *"I don't like your company's reputation!"*

- *"I don't trust you to deliver when promised!"*

- *"I don't like your quality standards!"*

Did you notice how specific these responses were? Many would think this is a GOOD thing because it means you can attack that objection and turn it around quickly. But in my experience, an objection (like the examples above) is NOT a good thing because it means you failed at one or more steps of the relationship building process. *In essence, an objection is a byproduct of a poor sales call.*

For example, if they object to your price you could have uncovered that earlier by finding out that "getting a lower price" was how the prospect "wins." But you failed to discover that because you probably rushed through that stage of the sales call so you could "get to the sale" and move on. There is always a fine line between being thorough and wasting the prospect's time. Only by making sales calls will you learn where that line falls and how not to go too far past it.

Your objection strategy is as follows:

Step One: What did I miss? Obviously, if you had followed the process correctly you wouldn't have missed their desire to get a lower price. But, what else may you have missed?

Because you didn't collect enough information and uncover needs the first time, you need to start from the beginning. I would not belabor points but you do need to clarify **Your Position** and the **Buyer's Position** if you hope to salvage this sales call. This means you should pick out one or two questions we discussed earlier and pull those out of your sales toolbox. Try to find out "what else," besides a lower price, is important to the prospect. If you can uncover just one new need then you can keep digging for gold.

Step Two: Summarize and Ask: Assuming you discovered at least one additional need (besides the one they objected to) you should now fall back into your sales "close" strategy. You will summarize what they said is important, remind them of the pain they will face if this need is not met, and ultimately ASK for the order again.

The worst thing that can happen at this point is they say "no" and you move on to another highly qualified prospect. You gave it your best shot of salvaging the call and that is all you can do as a salesperson. If the customer responds negatively to your objections strategy it's time to move on and find a better prospect. Remember, if you set up your sales funnel effectively you will have dozens of "hot leads" in your pocket and this prospect is just one of the many you will see this week or month.

In review . . .

"Finishing" the sales call means you are <u>asking for the order</u>. Done correctly, this should actually be the easiest part of the sales call because you have done all of the hard work. You created a budding relationship, you discovered common ground, you uncovered needs, and you presented your unique solution.

Whew! That's a lot of work! Sadly, most salespeople quit too soon. Believe or not, many salespeople get within a few feet of the "gold" but don't go further because of fear. According to the Sales Board Inc., only 38% of salespeople ASK for the order. This means that 62% of all salespeople have wasted their time and their company's resources having a conversation with no end game. Be bold, trust the relationship you built and simply ASK FOR THE ORDER!

Rules Buyers Are Taught

Depending upon the industry you are selling to, you may come across a professional buyer. Their role in the organization is to control their company's cash outflow through smart buying decisions.

Sometimes they focus on getting the price lower and sometimes they focus on just buying in smarter ways. If you are faced with this scenario, don't fret; professional buyers are still human beings who have needs you may be able to solve. If you use the *80/20 Selling Strategy* we outlined in earlier chapters, you can move along undeterred by their role.

Start by building rapport, find out your position, find out the buyer's position, and ultimately find out how they "win." Remember, professional buyers "win" in a variety of ways so you need to get to this point quicker than normal. The main reason for this is you do not want to waste YOUR valuable time with someone who "wins" by making you "lose." That's not how a healthy relationship begins and it will be destined for failure down the road.

The most common training tips I've witnessed for professional buyers involve the following:

1. **The first person to moves loses.** The best professional buyers show a true "poker face" during the entire selling situation. You can't read them very easily and that is to their advantage.

When it is finally time to present them with your offer, they will immediately reject it. Some do it so well and so convincingly that we think they are really offended, but believe it or not, this is a trained technique to win considerations or concessions from the desperate salesperson!

No matter what price you present, the buyer's knee-jerk reaction will be to tell you the price is too high. The best buyers will also react with a physical "flinch." This helps to cement the human reaction and the combination of words and body language will make most salespeople drop their price immediately.

Remember, the person with the most options has all of the power. YOU have all of the options because you have a well-oiled lead generation machine in place that is providing you solid leads each and every day.

Your strategy with this scenario (and it will happen sooner or later) is to "flinch" in reverse. If instead of reducing your price you say *"I'm sorry this is the best we can do, but if . . ."* The end of that sentence is *"but if . . ."* and you should fill that in by asking for something else.

In other words, *"I'm sorry this is the best we can do, but if you can guarantee us all of your orders for the year we can figure out a way to get the price in line with your needs."* Then, you should conclude with a closing statement such as, *"Can you guarantee us we will be your only vendor this year?"*

Do you see what you did? You turned a situation in which YOU were the patsy into a situation in which you were the most powerful person in the room!

What will this strategy do? It will either show you if they are serious about your solution or if they are merely looking for the lowest priced vendor. If the latter is the case, you can consider dropping your price, understanding it might be a weak foundation on which to begin your relationship. Of course you know what happens to a house built on a poor foundation; it eventually crumbles under pressure!

2.   **Reach for the moon . . . and take the stars too!** –
Professional buyers are often taught to "reach for the moon"
whenever possible. In essence, they are asking for more than
they ever expect to receive in return. For example, if short
delivery turnaround times are their key need, they will often
ask you for guaranteed fast delivery times along with
lowering the price just for the heck of it.

Why do professional buyers do this? Because
desperate salespeople will give in to their demands!
Remember, most salespeople are not great prospectors of
highly qualified leads. During a sales call the typical
salesperson is so excited just to be in the prospect's office
they will give away the farm because they don't know when
they will have this opportunity again.

If you just remember that YOU have the power and
YOU have options then you can leave your emotions at the
door. Your response to their ridiculous request is to either
oblige (not recommended), ignore the request beyond the
original agreement, or use the entire situation to your
advantage. This means you can "ask for the moon" in reverse
and ask for all of their business you can handle and first right
of refusal on items that may be outside of your typical product
line. Be bold and ask; you will be shocked at what they may
say! Worst thing that happens is they say no, and you're no
worse off than you were 30 seconds ago.

3.   **Bracketing for success.** One of my favorite TV shows is
the reality show about pawn shops called Pawn Stars. During
each episode, a person will bring in an item from home and
try to sell it to the pawn shop owner. Once they indicate their
desire to sell, the bracketing begins.

The word "bracketing" means exactly what it sounds
like. The buyer and the seller "bracket" the negotiation by

stating the high price (seller) and the low price (buyer). These two prices create a bracket in which the negotiations float back and forth until a final price is decided upon.

There are a few key rules in bracketing that must be followed if you expect to "win" this game. The first and most important rule that can NEVER be violated is:

NEVER make the first offer.

In other words, if you are the seller, you should initiate the conversation by saying, *"How much is this worth to you?"* The buyer (if they are untrained) will respond with a number and that will create the first "bracket."

By the way, if you are the buyer you would do the same thing in reverse. You would start the buying conversation by asking the seller, *"How much do you want for your product?"*

The person who responds first sets the first "bracket" no matter which side of the table they are sitting on. This is always the WEAKEST position in the negotiation process so NEVER make the first offer!

The second rule that you must understand in a bracketing situation is:

The negotiation always ends up in the middle.

For example, if the seller says, *"I want $100,"* then whatever number the buyer responds with will be the lowest end of the bracket.

Knowing that you are going to end up in the middle, you need to respond cautiously because you are in essence determining your future price. If you say, "$80," then you will probably end up paying $90 for the product. Therefore, if your goal is to truly lower the price you must establish a much lower bottom "bracket" number and start the negotiations from there. For instance, if you really want to pay $80, start at $60. Again, the reverse is true if you are the seller instead of the buyer; you would ask for much more to set a higher upper "bracket."

Bracketing prices is as old as time and has happened on every merchant street corner in every country in the world. The only caution to this approach is you can risk insulting the buyer or seller if you ask for too little or too high of a price. It totally depends on who has the most options and in this situation (which should be you).

If you think of this negotiating technique as a game, the better you will be. But if you go into it with dread and despair, it will keep you from selling from a position of power and ultimately leaving money on the table.

Finally, if you have a chance to watch Pawn Stars it will be well worth your time because you will see real life examples of bracketing being used. Or, if you are in a city where merchants sell their wares on the sidewalk I highly recommend you purchase something. These merchants do this every day and they are VERY good at what they do. But the lessons you will learn from them can make you thousands of dollars for years to come.

4. **Playing hard to get.** Prospects like this are the most dangerous prospects of all because they steal the most valuable asset you have: your TIME. There is NOTHING more precious than your time, and many salespeople are more than willing to deal with this because they assume it just comes with the territory. They assume you walk in, get "beat upon the head and shoulders," and hope the prospect feels sorry enough for you to buy something.

While many salespeople DO act in this way, none of the great ones do. Instead, the great salespeople know a prospect is a prospect is a prospect. No one prospect should matter anymore than another IF you are doing a good job generating leads.

The best way to overcome the prospect that is playing "hard to get" is to exhibit the same behavior. You probably didn't think I was going to say that, but think back to how human nature works in all aspects of our life.

If you were trying to get a date with the pretty girl in school you were probably faced with this attitude already. She knew she was the prettiest girl in school, and she knew YOU knew she was the prettiest girl in school. What kind of negotiating position do you think you were in at that point? Probably a weak one – and your body language showed it, which resulted in her either dismissing you altogether or "toying" with you until she was bored.

At some point she did go on a date and guess what type of boy she chose? Yeah, you guessed it, she chose the "bad boy." Why did she do this? <u>Because he acted disinterested in her!</u> He was the only one in school who didn't seem to care about whether he got a date with her or not, and guess what, he did! He turned the tables and he was now the one with the power.

I'm not saying that in sales you will always "get the date" but I am saying if you don't learn to project your power position at the right time you will be dismissed for another vendor. It may not happen immediately, but eventually they will get tired of playing with you and move on to someone that gives them at least the PERCEPTION of meeting their needs in a unique way.

5. **"I have ALL the power" technique.** With this approach you are combining two extremely powerful emotions – words AND actions. In this scenario you, the salesperson, made an offer and presented it to the prospect. In return, the prospect responded by not only giving you a stall or objection, but they SLID the offer back across the table to you.

This type of approach is famous in movies because of the power it exhibits. The person doing the sliding is like the silverback gorilla that is beating their chest and screaming loudly for all to hear. It's a power move, plain and simple.

Why do they do this?

You know the drill by now . . . they DO IT because they are faced with desperate salespeople each and every day. By making this "power move" to your initial offer they know the salesperson will often back down, even a little, and they have won the competition.

How do you handle this approach? Much like some of the earlier approaches, you can mirror their actions in reverse. You take the document they slid your way and, without looking at the offer a second time, you slide it BACK across the table and say, *"As far as I know, my offer is the best we can do . . ."*

If done correctly you are literally calling the prospect's bluff. The obvious danger of course is they weren't bluffing at all, and you just ended the sale altogether. But thankfully this really isn't a danger for an *80/20 salesperson* because YOU have more prospects than you can handle. YOU are keeping your emotions between a FIVE and SEVEN on the emotional scale and therefore this is just another prospect in your daily schedule. While this situation can elicit an adrenaline rush, do your best to keep your calm, never flinch, and wait for the results. If you did a good job uncovering needs, you'll have been in the driver's seat the entire time!

6. **"Give me ten estimates and a side of proposals please . . ."**

One of the classic stall techniques of professional buyers is to dump a mountain of proposal requests on the salesperson. To the untrained salesperson their initial reaction is, "They like me! They really, really like me!" But nothing could be further from the truth. Instead, they are showing you how they "win" and that a lower price is their goal. The buyer doesn't see how you're different from any competitor in your niche, BUT is thinking, *"If you give me the best price I would probably, maybe, switch over to your company."*

This technique happens often and when it happens to you, you have to make a choice based on the depth of the relationship you have built thus far. If you feel there are additional unmet needs (delivery times, lower price, higher quality, etc.) you CAN proceed with their request, but I would add the following twist.

Instead of taking their mountain of paperwork and spending countless hours creating proposals or estimates, I would simply say to them, *"In order to see if we are on the same page, please tell me which of these jobs is the most important to you, and I will prepare a proposal."* This twist turns the tables on them and will show you immediately if you have a chance at all to salvage this relationship. If they do pick out a single proposal then proceed as usual and pricing this job is the next event in your sales process. If they say, *"They are all equally important,"* I would walk away and move on to a better prospect.

The other technique you can use is to immediately remind them of the uncovered needs they discussed. Get them focused on those needs (instead of just price) and try to beat home the "pain and suffering" that will occur if those needs are unmet. If you feel you are making strides in this department, you can proceed by presenting a price and asking for an order <u>based on solving that most important unmet need.</u>

The final option you have involves creating a proposal for everything they offer you. If you go this route, I would make sure that there is enough money in the potential sale to justify your time. I would also "swing for the fences" in your final proposal instead of quoting each job individually. That means presenting your proposal as a "package," which will make it more difficult to price elsewhere.

When you quote something as a "package," it's like walking into a restaurant and asking to buy a cheeseburger. You would look at the menu, see ONE price, and make a decision to purchase or not. What you don't see is the price of the bun plus the price of the cheese plus the price of ketchup and so on. If you DID see this then your initial reaction would be, *"Boy, that ketchup is awfully expensive!"* which would invite more negotiating. For the restaurant, it would result in more lost sales than necessary.

When you sell a "package," your goal should be to group together both tangible and intangible services that are next to impossible to price out elsewhere. Done correctly, this creative approach can turn a lost sale into "home run" very quickly.

7. "But you don't understand . . ."

There are times during the closing stages of a sales call where the prospect or buyer will turn it into a "Dr. Phil" episode. What I mean by this is they will begin using THEIR problems as justification why they can't buy from you.

Most commonly, this will come in the form of a financial-based statement such as, *"We had a tough first quarter; we don't have the money to pay that price."* Instead of just telling you, *"Your price is too high,"* they brought in a personal reason to basically say, *"Your price is too high."*

So what do you do? Well, like all stalls and objections, you need to test for validity and the best strategy is to remind them, once again, of the needs they stated earlier. Next, remind them (once again), of the pain they will face if these needs are not met. Finally, ask a closing question such as, *"Are you ready to get started?"*

In my experience, when a prospect starts talking about the "gloom and doom" of their business, it is a huge "red flag" that they will be difficult to please for the life of your relationship. In these situations I prefer to move the call forward quickly, get to the uncovered need and ask one final buying question. If they don't bite I am looking for the door because, in my opinion, they have wasted enough of my valuable time already. Often, cutting your losses short and moving on to a better qualified prospect is the best move you can make!

8. Pinch an inch . . .

The best buyers are taught to "inch" or "nibble" just a little more from the seller. Typically this is done as soon as you consider the deal to be done. From the buyer's perspective, there is a HIGH probability that you, the salesperson, will give in to small concessions once you are convinced they will buy from you. In fact, this technique is almost never used until the deal is deemed to be final.

This approach is often subtle but it is just one more way for the buyer to "win" something from you so they can look great to their boss. They will often ask you to *"throw*

something in" for no extra money. Or, they will ask you to
"*speed up a delivery term.*" Or, they might ask for both to see
what they get!

You strategy to overcome this technique is to "inch"
in reverse. If they ask for a lower price, you should ask for a
larger chunk of what they purchase. If they ask for a quicker
delivery time, you should ask for a slightly higher price to
cover the overtime necessary to meet this new deadline. In
essence, you are using the bracketing technique we discussed
earlier. Like bracketing, you will probably end up in the
middle OR they will back off their request and you will end
up where you started with the original proposal. Either way, it
is okay to flex your sales muscle just a bit at this point.

9. Let me talk to my people . . .

Have you ever purchased a car? If so, you probably
witnessed multiple negotiating techniques throughout the
event. However, one tactic I guarantee you witnessed was the
"*let me talk to my people*" or "*let me talk to my supervisor*"
technique. This occurs when the salesperson leaves the car
lot, goes to a room and comes back to tell you, "*I would
LOVE to give you a better price but THEY won't let me.*"

Who are they? Well, "they" are that mysterious person
who has now taken on the role of disagreeing not only with
YOU, but with the salesperson too. This technique plays into
human nature because it tries to position the salesperson as an
ally. In other words, if it were up to him, he would certainly
give you that lower price; but "they" won't let him.

When you are making a sales call you will often face
this shortly after you ask for the order. The prospect will say,
"Let me run it by my people," in an attempt to avoid telling
you "yes" or "no." In reality, this situation should have been
discovered earlier in the information gathering stage but

regardless, you are faced with it now and must do something to salvage the call.

The best technique I have found to overcome this situation is to be bold and simply ask to have another sales call with all of the "people" in attendance. This technique will let you know how serious they are about their statement and it is the best way for you to translate the information directly to the real decision-makers.

If they say "no" to this request, your back-up strategy is to nail them down to a day and time by which they will have discussed with "their people." In reality, if they don't allow you to talk directly with the "people," you have probably lost this sale altogether. But if you would have uncovered the need for a committee review earlier in your sales call you wouldn't have wasted so much time with a weak lead! Chalk it up as a payment to the sales school of hard knocks and make a commitment not to coast through the early stages of a sales call ever again!

In Review . . .

Negotiating is just a way of doing business and it is something you should learn to appreciate. If you look at it as a game instead of personal attack on your proposal you will have more fun with the process.

Ultimately, the prospect still needs what your product or service offers and if you have graduated to the negotiation stage they are at least convinced you have an ability to meet some of their needs. Your job is to continually stress your value based on their spoken needs. From there, play along, find a happy medium, and turn that prospect into a long-term customer!

Creating 80/20 Value

In sales, not all approaches are created equal. This lack of equality is a result of the product you are offering and the value you must exhibit to turn a prospect into a customer. Just like in all facets of life, we must be "convinced" with different levels of influence depending upon how the purchase affects our overall personal (or business) budget.

For example, if you were hungry walking down the street and passed a hot dog stand, you would most likely stop, buy a hot dog and a Coke and move on with life. Did the hot dog stand operator have to convince you of the innate value of a hot dog and cool drink? Of course not! You had a need (hunger) and they had a product that could meet that need (food), and the signage grabbed your attention. This is sales in its simplest form and it works without any convincing at all because the product's value is very low.

Yes, the hot dog meets a basic human need but overall it is a low value product because you could substitute myriad other products and achieve the same purpose. The point with all of this is:

The <u>higher</u> the dollar value of the product, the <u>higher</u> value YOU must demonstrate.

This principle is based on human nature and EVERY prospect in the world will have a specific price level that they perceive as "high." Once your product's price hovers close to their "high" price, you need to demonstrate higher value to your prospect before you can convince them to buy.

What this means in reality is the sales cycle for higher value products tends to be **longer**. It may involve multiple steps that have the ultimate goal of turning the prospect into a customer. But you are literally selling in stages of ever-increasing value in order to get the prospect over the goal line at the end.

If you feel your product cannot easily be sold in a single selling event, don't fret; there is a process to overcome this challenge. The steps below can be altered slightly to meet your needs but the basic blueprint should not be changed because it has proven successful for the vast majority of my sales students.

Step One: Make the initial "face to face" sales call as normal. Once you get a qualified lead in your sales funnel, you must make an initial sales call as we spoke of earlier. The key difference here is you are going into the call with the full understanding that you are not selling a product today. Instead, you are selling a SECOND EVENT the prospect should agree to attend.

During the call you would proceed as normal with the questions that uncover needs. Again, the more needs you uncover the better, and if you fail to do this then you will be pushing a boulder uphill for the rest of the call.

Step Two: Once the needs are uncovered and the initial relationship is starting to build, it is time to start "selling" the next stage of the call, which is a higher value event. This higher value event should be something the PROSPECT deems as higher value than the initial sales call. In other words, it should meet the most pressing needs of the prospect and you should deliver it to them for FREE.

Think back to the conversation we had about selling drills. We discussed the importance of educating your customer on how to create a better hole! In your higher value event you should do the same thing.

The first thing you must do is establish what types of needs your prospects often have. This should be easy for you if you did the exercises earlier in the book. You know what your typical prospect will find important, and you'll use that information to create a higher value event that underlinetext{educates them} on solutions to that important need or needs.

For example, if you find out that ***"Time Constraints"*** are a common need of your prospect then you should offer to educate them on proper time management techniques. This could come in the form of either a videotaped presentation or a live event, preferably at your office.

The bulk of the presentation should be high value information that teaches them to plan their week, follow their schedule and avoid the interruptions that keep them from meeting their goals. You should actually give them enough information that they COULD do this on their own if they are willing to make massive changes in their daily habits. But *will* they make these changes? Probably not – and THAT is your golden ticket to a new customer.

During the higher value event you are literally showing customers the roadmap to a better future – with one caveat; you are ALSO showing them how hard it will be to travel this road alone. That is where YOUR better and easier-to-follow solution is shown to the prospect. You remind them of the challenges they deal with on a daily basis and then you show them a better way. Your solution offers a cleaner path that requires them to work LESS – if they give some of the workload to you and your team.

This selling approach is not done by many salespeople and it's because they don't understand that not all sales are created equal. They try to sell a $25,000 product the same way they would sell a hot dog. There is no relationship building process and as a result there is no trust equity built up. They simply uncover a few needs and ask for the order so they can move on to the next prospect.

BONUS STRATEGY:

If you are in a niche that has a higher dollar product offering, there is one other strategy I recommend. This strategy may not work for every niche, but if it does, this is an easier way to sell your end product.

In this strategy, you will take your main product and see if there are ways to break it apart. In other words, if your core product is a series of educational videos that cost $10,000, you could break these up into a three part series and sell them for less. Heck, you could break them up into a TEN part series – meaning the customer is making a $1,000 decision instead of a $10,000 decision.

The beauty of this method is it plays into human nature. Yes, the customer wants your product but they are not comfortable making a $10,000 decision just yet. If you can get them to say "yes" to something, anything, then you have a greater chance of selling them the core product.

Remember the old television commercials that used to sell you a _"Something of the month"_ subscription? Their ultimate goal was to sell you thirty collector spoons, or a bell with every state emblazed upon them, or a series of model train engines. They WANTED to sell you $1,000 or more worth of stuff, but they knew that if they had a television commercial about $1,000 worth of spoons, they would fail miserably. Therefore, they broke that up into smaller, more manageable bites and ultimately achieved the same goal by getting the customer to say "yes" once. That initial buy-in is a powerful tactic.

One final piece of their sales strategy involved sending you a display case where you would put each month's purchase for all to see. This is a beautiful marketing step because in the first month, all the consumer had was a display case with one lonely bell or spoon or train engine. The empty display case served as a 24-hour advertisement, reminding them of their need to keep their subscription active until it was filled up to completion.

This idea of "breaking up your product" is used by every successful marketer in the world from Tony Robbins to T. Harv Eker. They provide high levels of educational material that is loved by millions, but their ultimate money-making "goal" involves group education that costs $5,000, $10,000, $20,000 and up.

Many people don't realize this because they are focused on what they see in the infomercials: LOW dollar products like books or audio courses. These courses serve as the first "yes," which will ultimately get a percentage of their customers to the higher level buying the more expensive educational products.

If these masters of education only sold $10,000 courses how successful would they be? Not very, because they couldn't build the "value" necessary for you to make this type of decision by viewing a television commercial or visiting a website. Instead, they build "$29.95 worth of value" and give you an introductory product that far exceeds this price. They build trust equity by giving you tremendous value in return for a perceived low dollar item.

Naturally, the new customer looks at this and assumes, *"Heck, if they give me THIS MUCH for $29.95, I can't wait to purchase their $250 product!"* These low-risk purchases are the "gateways" that ultimately open the doors to more lucrative orders.

In the world of Neuro-Linguistic Programming or NLP, there is a 2-step process to become a master at something. NLP is a well-known process developed in the 1970's to speed up the mind / muscle connection to learning any task. It combines the neurological processes ("neuro"), language ("linguistic") and behavioral patterns from experience ("programming") to achieve goals quicker than ever.

1. Find someone who has ALREADY mastered the skills you   desire.

2. Do exactly what they are doing.

It really isn't any more difficult than that. All great marketers follow a pattern of breaking their higher dollar products into parts or steps and then sell these steps at ever increasing price points. Why not try to do the same thing in your business? It may make a tremendous difference without requiring a tremendous effort. In reality, selling the higher value items should get EASIER because you're working with customers who already know, like, and trust you. It's the 80/20 principle at work!

In Review . . .

Selling a higher value product takes more time and more energy – and sometimes more creativity. I encourage you to be creative and figure out a way to break your product into smaller and more manageable pieces. By doing this you will hear "yes" more times and can keep selling at higher levels of value. Ultimately, selling WILL become easier because you are literally selling "hot dogs" to a hungry person; which is the best kind of customer to build your

business upon – the one who doesn't even have to think twice about the purchase!

Creating an 80/20 Sales Team

Building a staff of great workers is always hard, and if you had to choose the hardest role to fill, my guess is it would be that of the salesperson. The problem that most business owners face when searching for great salesperson is the lack of knowing what they want, coupled with the lack of training.

If you were hiring for other positions in your business, you are typically assured the person is trained to do their job. For example, if you want a new bookkeeper, you will find that all who apply are already familiar with accounting principles and accounting software. They come to you prepared for their jobs, but with salespeople this is rarely the case.

Most salespeople were not properly trained to do their job in the first place. In fact, most of them started in another role and grew into sales over time. This could have been because of their company's needs or the salesperson's desire to make more money and live the glamorous "sales life." Whatever it was, most salespeople were simply given leads (or not) and thrown into the water to learn how to swim.

The salespeople who lasted longer than six months figured out how to swim. They either learned how to say the right things or tap the right people. Whatever it was that got them past the six month point, it worked. Was it the best way for a salesperson to operate? Probably not, but desperation leads to desperate actions and while you can mow a lawn with scissors it's not the best way to do it! They were merely trying to survive so they figured out the quickest way (in their minds) to get from point "A" to point "B" with the only skill sets they possessed.

The first rule of hiring a great sales team is to make sure you are hiring to COMPLEMENT your activities. In any business, the leader is always the most powerful salesperson the moment they walk in the door. The prospect knows they can "make it happen" quicker than any other person. This is a power position that cannot be duplicated. But as your business grows, your role as chief salesperson may diminish as you take on other tasks. That is the point where you should look to hire other representatives who will continue what you have already started.

There are several keys to hiring salespeople that should never be violated. These are fundamental principles, and done correctly, give you the best chance of assembling a great team. Skip a step and you will see failure more times than not.

Key Point #1: YOU provide the sales plan

The first pitfall that most owners run into is hiring a salesperson without a plan in place. Remember, how you sell should always start with you, the owner. You need to be the "feet on the street" and you need to see a prospect's face when you make certain statements. If you fail to do that, you are going to bring in a salesperson and throw them in the water to see if they can swim. Good luck!

The plan you create should be based on your personal experiences in the field. It should also be a WRITTEN plan. This means you should explain how leads are generated, what the salesperson needs to do first / second / third and what they should specifically say in each situation. The more specific you can be with a new salesperson, the better chance they have for success.

Some of you are reading this and you immediately think this violates the "free thinking" salesperson approach portrayed by Hollywood. But Hollywood is not real life; in reality the best salespeople are HIGHLY trained and they follow a step-by-step formula every day of their sales life.

So, what is your sales plan? If you can't write it down in easy-to-follow steps you aren't ready to hire a new salesperson. Do not violate this principle – ever!

Key Point #2: Give 'em 90 days . . .

Earlier I said that a worker will be the best they will ever be in the first 90 days of their employment. I'm not saying they won't develop further and be more valuable as time goes on, but their BEHAVIOR and ACTIVITIES levels will be the best they will ever be in those initial three months.

With this being said, you should focus your sales training as an intense 90-day period of performance. Selling is unlike any other activity at your business and it is rare for a salesperson to produce real tangible results in 90 days. But what they can do is perform their activities at the highest level possible. Therefore, what you are judging them on in those first three months is their ACTIVITY LEVEL and not necessarily their RESULTS. You want to see them following your plan to the letter each and every day of their employment.

The best sales plans involve pre-qualified leads coming to the salesperson on a daily or weekly basis. This is the goal but this should not be the starting point for your new salesperson. Instead, you should start with the activity that is most important to all salespeople: "dialing for dollars." While this is NOT the long term path to success you still must develop good communicators so think of this step as an initiation or a training exercise. Regardless of how you frame it, the best salespeople are great prospectors because they learn to take small bits of information and dig deeper to turn that into new business down the road. They turn one lead into three by communicating and asking the right questions. This is a learned skill that starts with talking to people every day.

Day One to Thirty . . .

Day ONE to day THIRTY should involve the salesperson calling through lists of potential prospects using a script that YOU have developed. You don't want to turn these "green" reps loose on great leads; instead focus their activities on one of the following:

- Old prospects that never turned into a customer. While these may be harder to make contact with they will be a great exercise in getting through the "gate keeper" on the other line. These are lessons that will pay dividends for years to come.

- Dormant customers who stopped buying from you at some stage. This is something that happens to all businesses from time to time and it is usually a result of your business not staying in touch with your customer. We look up one day and wonder where they went. That's how a customer leaves you; not kicking and screaming but instead they remain silent long enough until you don't remember them at all. Don't let that happen to you!

- Dormant jobs that were purchased in previous years but haven't been purchased this year. Like dormant customers, we often have dormant jobs from existing customers. This means that we still have the customer but they are only buying at 50% of the level of the previous year. This happens for a variety of reasons but improving your communication can help you find out why and begin to regain that work.

For the first 30 days, focus your new salesperson on contacting prospects from these three groups. There is little fear of the salesperson doing harm because in all three circumstances you are making no money from these prospects anyway!

Day 31 to 60

On day thirty one it is time to add something to the new salesperson's plate. For the next thirty day period you should continue to focus their activities on prospecting to the three groups. But in addition to that, you should now allow them to go on a JOINT sales call with a more experienced rep; preferably to a prospect the new salesperson called. This will begin to show the new salesperson the results of their calls. It will show them if they are doing a good job at finding out if the prospect really wants a sales call or if they just said "yes" to get the new salesperson off the phone.

Additionally, by bringing the new salesperson on sales calls they will start to learn your sales process. They will hear the scripts in action and see how the experienced salesperson handles stalls, objections, and gripes. They will see how the experienced salesperson creates unique solutions, positions his company as different from other competitors and focuses on items OTHER than price. This mentoring exercise will move the new salesperson to a higher level and they will start to get their "feet wet" without having to know how to swim solo just yet.

Day Sixty-One to Ninety

The final thirty day proving period will increase the new salesperson's role once again. Now in addition to making prospecting calls to the three customer groups above, the new salesperson will either go on a sales call SOLO or have a JOINT call but act as the lead salesperson. Whether you send them out solo or in tandem with an experienced rep is up to you. But it is vital they take the lead during the call so they can "feel the heat" and respond accordingly.

What happens on day ninety one?

On day ninety one you have a choice to make. You can either keep the new salesperson longer or you can make them available to the industry. You should make this decision based upon the ACTIVITIES they exhibited for the first 90 days. If they performed at a high level, I would keep them around and develop them further. But if their attitude and progress were sub-par, I recommend you move on to a new salesperson.

It's a shame to waste ninety days on a weak worker but the reality is most companies waste six months or more before they make the decision to terminate. The reason this occurs is typically because the company didn't have a sales plan in place to begin with. When the new salesperson started, the company floundered for a month or two and wasted both their time and the new salesperson's time. Don't let that be you. Start with a plan, follow that plan, and create an 80/20 salesperson for your business!

80/20 Networking . . . or is it NOT working?

Networking is often confused with NOT working and again, this occurs because a plan never existed. Most owners and salespeople view networking as a chance to escape their day, mingle with a few business friends and have a drink or two. They also misconstrue this activity as "making sales calls" and they pat themselves on their backs because of the sales activities they accomplished this week.

In fact, they often use "networking" as the ONLY sales path for their company. While this can work and it can bring in some business, it is not a true sales plan. Most business professionals network the way an amateur fisherman fishes. They get in the "boat" (go to the networking event), cast their rod (say "hi" to a few people at the event), and hope for the best.

This type of networking is not only a waste of your sales time but it is not an 80/20 activity. In fact, if I am working with a business owner and they list "networking" as one of their sales activities, the next thing I would ask them to do is rank its effectiveness. In my mind "effective" is anything that turns into money quickly. When the business owner is honest, they rarely list "networking activities" higher than a two or three on my five point scale. This means it is a very weak activity in terms of turning time into cash. But it doesn't have to be that way!

Why Network?

Networking, done correctly, can expand your marketing reach by building key relationships and presenting your value. It is one of the few ways you can influence people just with your presence. More importantly, it is done in a casual environment which makes it easier to have value-laced conversations without the stigma of trying to make a sales call.

The keys to making your networking experience the most valuable hour of your life requires you to sharpen your skills BEFORE you go to the event. Once there, it's too late to plan your strategy; this must be done beforehand and practiced to perfection. Finally, the real key to networking properly is learning how to carry a conversation. Some of you reading this are natural conversationalists and this will come naturally. If that is not you, don't fret; carrying a conversation is a learned skill.

Networking Misconceptions

Think back to your last networking event. If you are like most networkers you acted in one of two manners. You either:

1. **Sat by yourself, most likely in the corner of the room.** This is the typical strategy of most networkers. They come to the event, go straight to the bar or buffet to grab a plate of food, and then head to the corner to finish up their time. They look at networking almost like a prison sentence and they are just counting down the minutes until it is over.

In their minds, if someone sits beside them and a conversation starts this is a successful networking event. But we all know that this is a waste of your time and if you were really applying 80/20 to your sales process you would either make the most of this event OR you wouldn't be there at all. If you don't come with a plan to canvas the room you might as well pick another sales strategy altogether.

2. **You come to the event and hang around the same two or three people every week**. This type of person has graduated from sitting in the corner alone but they aren't

doing much better. Instead, they find their two friends, talk about their past week's experiences and wait for the event to be over.

If this is your strategy you are still in the "not working" category. While existing relationships are important, to truly network you must continually build NEW relationships. You should think of each new person you meet as a potential salesperson who will share your value with somebody else. Done correctly, it's like having a walking billboard in the business world that will tell your story to others and pre-sell you to prospects. This is the best situation you can be in, because they did the hardest part of warming up the lead ahead of your visit.

Finally, what you THINK you are doing and what you are actually doing in a networking event are often two different things. We all give ourselves more credit than we deserve. In our minds, we typically turn a "good" job into a "great" job. It's sort of like the fishing story where the fish you caught keeps getting bigger as the years pass on. Most of us are not natural networkers. If we understand that from the beginning, then we know we need to do something about it. Here are the most common networking misconceptions I find with my coaching clients.

I tried it once . . . it doesn't work

Like most of sales in general, it takes consistency and a solid plan of attack to see results. Networking is no different because it also requires consistency and a solid plan to be successful. Later on, I will teach you a plan that works – but just know that YOU must put in the time to be successful. Not only must you practice your skills ahead of time while nobody is looking, you must also practice them out in the field. If you've ever played sports, you know exactly what I'm talking about.

For example, in golf, there are thousands of men and women who play golf at a PGA or LPGA level . . . on the driving range! They strike the ball crisply, the rarely miss their target, and their swing looks picture-perfect. However, 99% of them (and maybe more) couldn't do this regularly under the heat of competition. This is why they must take their "driving range swing" and apply pressure to see how it reacts. In the same way, you must take your polished networking approaches out in the field to see how you do under the "heat" of competition. What sounded good in front of the mirror may not get the same reaction when you say it to another person!

Everyone already knows me . . .

While many in your networking group may know who you are and who you work for, they rarely understand exactly what you can offer them. I know this for a fact because I've been involved with sales calls in which I reminded the prospect (or customer) of something we spoke about six months ago and they reacted by saying, "I didn't know you could do that!"

We all know what happens when we assume something and this could never be more dangerous than when we assume our prospect truly "knows" us. That would mean they know us from inside out and they truly understand the value we can bring them; which is rare.

In earlier chapters I mentioned that it takes as many as seven times before a prospect notices your advertisement. The same applies to networking and exchanging your value with the prospect. In reality, you can't remind them enough because whatever is important to them at that very minute is what they will remember. If it isn't important to them, they will dismiss it and forget you ever said it. But the salient point to remember is that they WILL have a need for your product or service someday – and when the time comes you need to be the vendor on their speed dial!

Networking is manipulative . . .

Those who have this view are probably not cut out to be salespeople in the first place because they most likely think ALL selling is manipulative. For networking specifically, think of it as **small talk with a purpose**. That purpose of course is to begin or build a budding relationship that will ultimately turn into a paying customer as you both find value in each other. Their needs and your abilities will mesh as is the case with all GOOD relationships.

Remember, most of us think of sales or networking based on the worst experiences we've ever had. We then translate that negative experience of the pushy salesman or sleazy networker to all sales or networking activities, which keeps us from reaching our goals. All business in the world was built on relationships in some way, shape, or form. After all, it's tough to sell anything to a customer who doesn't trust you. And since relationship-building is a crucial for business, you need to get good at it!

Networking is just "schmoozing"

Unfortunately, this is mostly true because most of the attendees have no clue how to properly network. You are typically surrounded by salespeople who are only there for the drinks and munchies. But just because THEY don't understand how to properly network doesn't mean you can't be an all-star at the event.

Instead of thinking of "schmoozing" as a negative, you should use it to your advantage. Because of the casual atmosphere at most networking events, you can more easily enter conversations with strangers. You can also find out more about them in a shorter time frame than normal IF you have a plan! While most attendees are "schmoozing" you can be digging for needs or pain points and then use that information at the appropriate time to achieve your ultimate goal.

I don't need any favors right now so why bother?

If you look at networking (or sales) as an opportunistic event, you will have a difficult time in business. The best salespeople and the best networkers build their plan on reciprocity. This valuable exchange should involve meeting needs by both parties but it starts with you, the vendor. Your primary job at a networking event is to build a relationship in the same way personal relationships are built. You should seek to uncover needs, giving of yourself and growing the relationship in stages, just like you would do with a new friend.

Networking is just handing out business cards to strangers

Yes, you need to have appropriate "leave behinds" that keep your message in front of your prospect. But blanketing them with business cards or any other media is not your primary purpose. The person who leaves the event with the most business cards DOES NOT WIN. In fact, that person probably loses each and every time!

Within a networking event, you are better served to hand ONE or TWO business cards to prospects <u>at the appropriate time</u> than to hand out twenty business cards in a harried fashion. The 80/20 rule applies each and every time to passing out business cards and your goal is to make sure it is a TOOL that complements the conversation and not a WEDGE that interrupts it.

When a person hands you a business card what do you do with it? What is your next step? This is part of the planning process that turns "small talk" into "small talk with a purpose." If you do not have a follow-up plan that involves taking that business card and using it to create a valuable relationship, then why get the card in the first place? So, what's your plan? Keep reading and I'll give you my recommended follow up procedure for success!

Sharpen Your Networking Skills

If you want to be great at any activity, you must start with a solid understanding of the fundamentals. From there, you must practice these fundamentals to perfection. They must become second nature or they won't show up when they are needed most. Instead, what WILL show up under pressure is what feels the most comfortable to you. In networking, that typically means you shrink off into a corner and wait for the event to end.

To be a great networker you must understand networking fundamentals and sharpen those skills to perfection. The following skill-sets are the holy grail of networking and if you desire to be the best, you need to duplicate what the best networkers do. Here are the networking fundamentals that help them perform each and every time:

Learn to Talk to Strangers

From the time we were a child we were taught one key rule of survival: "don't talk to strangers." I'm sure your mom or dad said this to you many, many times and they did their best to strike fear into you if you ever dared to break this rule. Of course mom and dad meant well; they were doing this because they wanted the best for you and wanted you to be safe. Unfortunately, what they also did is set in motion a learned behavior that many people take into adulthood.

Talking to strangers is the key to expanding your business network and it's the key to business survival. In business, we will all lose a percentage of business from our current customers through no fault of our own. They will go out of business, sell their companies, or hit an economic pothole that causes their sales to dip dramatically. Regardless of the reason, it is not IF it happens but WHEN it happens. You WILL lose sales from your existing accounts this year, I guarantee it! Statistically I find this loss to be in the 5% to 8% range on average. This means the first 5% of new sales you bring in this year will REPLACE last year's attrition.

What is the answer to this? Well, expanding your network of course! You must always plant in the spring to harvest in the fall. The worst thing you can do as a business leader is to wait until the sales are lost before you do anything about it. Taking this approach is like the farmer walking out to their field for the fall harvest and going, "Oops, I forgot to plant in the spring!" At that point it's too late and you are left to wait for the sales cycle to pop out new customers, which could result in many cold months ahead!

Talking to strangers is not just a fun activity you should learn. It is as vital as breathing and it is truly the air that fills a business' lungs. Without it, your company will eventually lose energy and will eventually cease to exist. The good news is all of this is highly foreseeable and highly preventable, but it does require you to talk to strangers!

Enter a room enthusiastically!

Earlier we discussed the importance of positive body language. That could never be truer than during a networking event. Your entire body is out for the world to see and you can't even cover half of it by sitting behind a desk! Therefore, you must be aware of this fact and, more importantly, have a plan of attack to put your best foot forward.

Step One: Energize Yourself! When you enter a room people are watching. Maybe you think you can sneak in without them noticing but somebody WILL notice and they will immediately form an opinion of you. Take this a step further and apply it to entering a circle of people at a networking event. This happens frequently and if you enter the circle with a smile on your face and a light in your eyes, you have the best chance of being received in a positive manner.

Your body language will "sell" you way before you utter your first word; make sure it is selling the most positive version of you possible. From here, take this head start and build upon it to create the beginnings of a new relationship. But if you don't look like a person they would want to relate with, then you have already lost the game before you said a word!

Step Two: Don't Be Too Serious! We have all met this type of networker. They have taken their goal of "small talk with a purpose" to a whole new level. They missed out on the most important part of this process, which is to build a relationship. They are so focused on getting to the goal line that they don't enjoy the game at all. More importantly, the people they encounter don't enjoy playing the game with them either!

We all spend our days with way too much seriousness. The last thing we want is to spend our networking time being bombarded by seriousness at a time when we are involved with one of the least serious sales activities of all.

Ideally, if you were being videotaped at a networking event, you would get two different perspectives depending upon where the camera was located in the room. If it were far away and panning the crowd you should stand out by your positive body language. If the camera stopped at you for a minute or two, it would appear you were involved in a casual conversation where both parties were enjoying themselves.

Take this a step further and now the camera is up close and personal. It can not only see you but can record the conversation as well. It would still see a casual conversation between two parties who seemed to like each other, but it would also observe far more. It would observe you, the all-star networker, building a relationship by asking good questions. No, you are not peppering your "victim" until they relent and turn over the valuable answers. Instead, you are naturally giving AND taking which is how all relationships are built. The end result is two interested parties who will exchange particulars and probably plan to talk again in the near future.

E.N.G.A.G.E. Your Audience.

Using the two foundational steps above will get you noticed (in a positive way), but they are only door openers. It is now up to you to position yourself for success by engaging your audience in an interesting but positive manner. To help you along in this process I use the E.N.G.A.G.E model that I've learned from others over the years. This model is a great acronym to help you under pressure.

Establish Eye Contact: While this applies to all selling and conversational situations it doesn't apply any more powerfully than during a networking event. We have all been on the receiving end of poor eye contact and we remember it because of the negative feeling it gave us. Eye contact, when used correctly, is never noticed by the receiving party. We leave these types of conversations with a good feeling about the other person; we know they cared about what we were saying but we can't point to anything in particular.

On the flip side, when we are the victim of poor eye contact we immediately have "bad vibes" about the individual. More importantly, it will be extremely difficult for us to let them proceed further in the sales process. Our bias radar will kick in and they will have to jump through many hoops to sell us on their services. Or, we may stop trying to sell them on our services even though they may be a tremendous prospect. We've talked about body language before but this simple yet powerful habit (good or bad) can make all the difference in our relationship building process!

Nodding (appropriately): One of the strongest positive body language signals (after eye contact) is nodding in agreement. It is human nature to like a person who agrees with us, even when we are wrong. The act of nodding is a positive affirmation that you agree with the person talking.

Combine nodding with fixed eye contact and the other party will walk away from the conversation thinking you are an all-star networker! More importantly they will WANT to seek you out or take your calls because something in their gut tells them that you care about what they are doing. It is a powerful accelerator in the relationship building process and the best networkers and salespeople use this technique every day. Why wouldn't you do the same?

Geniality: If you search for this word's definition you will find it to say, "The quality of having a friendly and cheerful manner." In our life we have people who are bubbling with geniality and those who are not. Which type of people do you desire to spend the most time around? The former of course. If you were dreading a visit to a customer – or even a visit to a family member's house – it was probably because they lacked geniality.

People are naturally drawn to others who are friendly or cheerful because all of us have enough gloom and doom in our lives already. The last thing we want to do is to willingly choose more! Make sure you have a good attitude the moment you walk into a networking event or a sales call.

Even if your personal world is falling down around you, make it a point to leave that emotional baggage at the door. Picture yourself in the attitude you would exhibit if things WERE going your way. The good news is that human nature reacts to how we THINK, which changes how we FEEL, which changes how we ACT. If you change the way you THINK you will ultimately change the way you ACT and long-term that will change your destiny. But it all starts with YOU!

Aim Your Attention: Like eye contact and nodding, aiming your attention on the person who is speaking will further cement your reputation as one who cares about them. Aiming your attention involves positioning your body so that it faces the speaker. Many people (especially men) have the habit of standing shoulder to shoulder with the person speaking. Their belt buckles are often facing in the SAME direction. For whatever reason, this is a natural habit but that doesn't mean it is a good habit. Learn to face the speaker and they will think you truly care about what they are saying.

While we are on the subject about facing the speaker, let us assure we are paying attention to personal space. All humans have an imaginary buffer around them that they deem as their "personal space" and they do not want it to be penetrated. In my research I have found that space to be about three feet in diameter or about the length of an extended arm. While everyone is different, this is a general rule of thumb I would use in each and every conversation. Like poor body language, invading someone's personal space will leave them with uneasy feelings about you.

Gesture Appropriately: Gesturing, when done correctly, is never noticed. It complements the conversation and adds to the building of a relationship. The best way to gesture is by imagining a box around your torso. Your goal is to never let your hands leave that box. It is when hands start climbing above or to the left or right of the box that gesturing can become a distraction to the conversation. Do it too much, and the speaker will start to follow your hands and either get off track or stop listening to what you have to say.

A common and powerful gesturing technique that many salespeople use is the ***Mirroring Technique***. This is when you begin to duplicate the gestures of the person you are talking to. For example, if they cross their arms you will naturally cross yours. If they put a finger on their chin you do the same. One word of caution here, if you don't make NATURAL moves it will become obvious to the other party and will derail the entire point of this technique. Use good judgment, mirror when appropriate, and don't overdo it!

Easing Your Posture: If we expect the other person to engage us appropriately, we can't be too stiff or robot-like. We have to be a human who is having a conversation with another human. This means that while we shouldn't slouch or hunch over, we do need to make natural movements with our arms and shoulders. Be loose in the same way you would be loose in front of a trusted friend. Make yourself approachable and then once approached, make yourself to be a person they would like to be around further.

There you have it, the basics of learning to E.N.G.A.G. E. with your audience.

Establish Eye Contact

Nodding

Geniality

Aim Your Attention

Gesture Appropriately

Ease Your Posture

Breaking Into a Networking Circle the 80/20 Way!

One of the unspoken fears of networking is the fear of being left out of the conversation or circle. If you could take a "bird's eye" view of the scene at a networking event you would see small circles of people engaged in conversation. If you are one of those people in a circle, you feel as if you fit with the crowd and that gives you a sense of accomplishment. But what happens if you are NOT part of the circle and want to join in on the conversation? Well, there's a process for that and it works each and every time!

The first step to successfully joining a group is to use your powers of observation. Ideally you would spot at least one person in the group who you already have familiarity with. This helps ease the transition into the group and human nature will make you more acceptable because you are "in the know" with a member of the group.

Now that you have chosen your group, it is time to engage them using a very simple yet powerful process. As you approach the group, approach opposite the speaker. This means you shouldn't sneak up behind them and end up shoulder to shoulder with the speaker. Doing this can cause the speaker to be startled by you and it will most likely interrupt the conversation altogether. Always approach so the speaker can see you coming their way!

As you approach the group you will probably be faced with a major physical obstacle which is the closed circle of the group. Human beings tend to form in groups during social activities and instinctively create physical barriers that separate their group from the rest of the crowd. It's a state of nature, but if you desire to be a part of the group you need to be able to break into the group in a tactful way.

After researching the various ways one can enter this closed circle situation, I have found that the easiest way is to approach the circle and then gently touch the ELBOW of one of the people in the circle. When you do this a magical thing happens; the circle opens up! Again, it's a state of nature. Don't fight it but instead use it to your advantage!

As the circle opens up make sure you keep a smile on your face and eye contact with the speaker. Additionally, find one other person within the group and make eye contact with them as well. This exhibition of positive body language will help you get accepted into the group without uttering a word.

Now that you are officially part of the new group the last thing you want to do is rock the boat. Therefore, make your first mission to listen to the person speaking and to NOT interrupt. Let the speaker finish their story and let others respond if necessary. After this, there should be a natural time for you to engage and I recommend you speak directly to the person you are most familiar with OR the person who let you into the group. Introduce yourself and ask an appropriate question to start a conversation. The rest should flow from here.

Remember Names in 5 Seconds . . .

The key to remembering names is to focus for those few brief seconds and to extend the introduction just a bit longer. In order to do this you should:

1. **Repeat the first name** – For example, upon meeting the person for the first time you should say, *"Hi Jennifer, it's so nice to meet you."* By doing this you will now hear the name twice within a span of a few seconds. This helps to cement their name in your mind.

2. **Ask for the last name again (or confirm)** – Again, the purpose of this is to extend the introduction until their particulars are burned into your brain. You can either say, *"And your last name was . . .?"*

3. **Ask a comment or question about their name** – This final step should seal the deal for you and will greatly assist in remembering the name. An example of this approach is: *"Do you like to be called Jenny or Jennifer?"*

Now that you know THEIR name, how are you going to get them to remember YOUR name? Again, we have a plan for that:

1. **Give them a "double dip"** – Like you did with their name, you need to extend your introduction just a bit and a great way to do this is by "double dipping," which means repeating your name in the span of a few seconds. For example, you could say, *"My name is John. John Smith."*

2. **Separate and articulate** – Because we all speak at different speeds it also means we interpret information at different speeds. Therefore, we need to start off by speaking SLOWER and assuring we articulate each word. If you did this properly with your introduction you would say, *"My name is John. John (pause) Smith."*

3. **Make your name memorable** – This last part is totally optional but if done correctly, they will never forget your name. A great example of this would be, *"My name is Nancy Mann, that's Mann with two 'n's'. I'm the only woman who's a Mann in real estate in Kansas City."* While not everyone is willing or able to easily do this, I suggest you give it a try if you want to stand out from the crowd!

Answering the "Big Three"

In every networking or social event there are three main <u>unspoken</u> questions that need to be answered:

1. Who you are?

2. What do you do?

3. What are we going to talk about?

When you are answering the "what do you do" and "who are you" questions you must be careful because most of us answer these questions in four ways – none of which are helpful for our long term success. The first way we answer the question is by labeling ourselves based on our industry or job duty. For example:

- I'm a plumber

- I'm a salesman

- I'm a writer

These types of questions will often fall like a bag of cement. More importantly, they will squash out any conversation because the other party will probably respond with an, *"Oh, that's nice,"* type of response. Bam! Conversation over!

If you don't respond by labeling yourself you will often wave the company flag by going in the opposite direction and giving out TOO much information. People who respond this way will say things like, *"I'm Assistant Information Systems Manager with the Masters Division of Management Information Systems, Inc."* Again, this is a conversation killer because you probably lost the other person somewhere after "information systems" and they probably didn't hear the rest. Again, their response will probably be, *"Oh, that's nice."*

The third way to end the conversation before it begins is by identifying the industry or market niche you are in. Examples would be:

- I'm in real estate

- I own a restaurant

- I'm in consulting

Thud! Conversation over – another wasted opportunity!

The final way we poorly introduce ourselves is by being too vague. We don't define WHAT we do at all. Like a fog on a city, we have put a fog on ourselves and it's a conversation killer. Examples of this would be:

- I'm with XYZ corporation

- I work at Jones & Associates

While your company may be unique in your mind it is rarely that way in the eyes of others. The only way this approach would make sense is if your company is well known AND they do one key task (like accounting) that couldn't be misconstrued. These are big risks to take and more times than not, you will fail to carry a conversation after making this introduction.

Now that you know what NOT to do, let's learn what to do. As you build your introduction you need to decide if it is a conversation *BUILDER* or a *STOPPER*. The best way to learn this is by practicing it in public, but you can give it the best chance of success by following these rules.

The first sentence of your introduction should tell what you do BEST. For example:

"I take the pain out of buying or selling your home"

Next, you should continue by using a real world example of how you helped a specific customer do exactly what you said you did. For example:

". . . In fact, I just helped a customer sell their home in 45 days for 5% above market value."

Your ultimate goal is for the prospect to say:

"Wow! Tell me MORE!"

The "tell me more" response is how you know your introduction worked to perfection. You now have your hook in the prospect and it's up to you to keep the conversation flowing by answering the last unspoken question which is, *"What are we going to talk about?"*

Most conversations at business events go like this:

"Hi, how are you?"

"Good, How are you?"

"Not bad. What's new?"

"Not much. What's new with you?"

"Not much. Been real busy."

"Me too. We'll get together sometime."

"Great idea. I'll give you a call."

"Okay, bye. See you later."

Did this sound familiar? If you are honest with yourself it probably does, but it doesn't have to be that way! Here's how to overcome this obstacle:

1. **Start with an agenda**: This means you need (you guessed it) to have a PLAN before you walk in the door. This plan should involve what you want to GIVE and what you want to GET.

To give properly you need to think of ways you can <u>make their lives easier</u>. This could be by introducing them to another person, offering them a free service or answering a key question. Giving is the easiest way to start the relationship process!

On the flip side, what you want to GET should help you move towards your overall goals of getting more customers. This could be an introduction to a new prospect or an answer to a nagging question that only they can answer. Bottom line, have a plan that involves BOTH giving and receiving!

2. **Look for cues (openings)**: During the course of the conversation you should be aware of natural cues or openings that allow you to implement your plan in Step #1. The more natural the better and it must be a <u>natural part</u> of the overall conversation!

3. **Use success stories to tell what is new:** This is a great way to not only market what you do but start a great conversation. People are always interested in new information and by talking about your latest expansion, new office building, or an award you received, you can fill both needs. Always have a story or two in your back pocket but don't hog the conversation. Ask them what's happening in THEIR world too!

In review . . .

Networking, done correctly, can be the easiest way to make a large number of contacts in a very short period of time. But you must have a plan of attack for every situation you will run into. If you do the hard work now, this new skill-set will be one that can bring your sales and your business to the next level!

80/20 Future Planning

Planning for your business's future is easier than you think. Sure, you can't control the environment or economic turbulence, but you can put yourself in the best position to succeed IF you use your past experiences to shape your future behaviors.

All of your future planning should center on your customer base TODAY. While it is good to consider what you "hope and dream" to do there is nothing more powerful than what you are already doing. We all know that the 80/20 within the 20% is the most powerful mathematical advantage we have, so we need to use it for our future planning too.

Begin your planning by analyzing the TOP 5% of your customers ONLY. Statistically these customers should represent 50% or more of your overall sales. Assuming this is true in your situation, it is time to analyze this list further. One word of caution: at the end of this exercise you may be faced with the stark reality that you should change your model in drastic ways. Many business owners fight this because they look at changes (like reducing staff) as a step back. This could not be further from the truth.

Step One: What Equipment Do You Need?

The first stage of deciding your future is to take a deep look at what you use to produce your product. This is often a hard item to look at because, if you are like most businesses, you are covered with layers of equipment that has been collected over the years to handle customer demands. The problem however, is that you were handling the demands of the mass of customers who really don't contribute much to your overall success! This is a common trap that all business owners fall into, but you can break out of it.

When deciding to get rid of equipment, don't think of it as a step back; instead it is an evolution to the next level. Evolution of businesses is necessary for them to survive and like all evolutionary processes; we have to make decisions that are radically different than the decisions that got us here.

A few generations ago, digging a ditch used to involve a dozen men with shovels and a period of days or weeks. Then, lo and behold the evolutionary process created a backhoe that could easily replace the workload of ten men with shovels.

Somebody had to make this evolutionary step in their business and at the time, it probably wasn't a popular choice because it put men out of work. But it broke a barrier in the speed of digging a ditch that allowed many of the structures we have today. Without making this leap, many other processes wouldn't have evolved easily either. We MUST evolve based on the technology available to us at the time. You can "***do more with less***" today than ever before if you don't get stuck in old paradigms!

Using your top 5% customers as a guide, decide which equipment in your facility is required to handle this work. Does ALL of your equipment contribute to their work? Probably not. Does 90% contribute? 80%? 70%? Only you can decide but if you are like most businesses, you can probably remove 30% or more of your equipment and still handle the workload of your top 5% customers who contribute 50% or more of your overall sales.

Now take this a step further and eliminate the overhead expenses of this unnecessary equipment. This means the monthly payments, the maintenance costs, the repair bills and so forth. Does that make a serious dent in your overall budget? Does it free up a great deal of cash? As you can see, we are beginning to challenge the old assumptions of what you truly need to run your business.

Finally, the question you are probably wondering is how you are going to handle the remaining 50% or more of your customer's work without equipment. Well, you have two choices to handle this quandary. The first choice is to find a better, more evolutionary way to produce the work without the equipment. For many, there ARE other ways to do the same job if we think outside of the box. Additionally, you could also look at joint ventures or partnerships with other vendors who could do this type of work and you would act as a reseller. For some of you this is possible and for others it is not, but if you CAN take this approach, I highly recommend it.

The second choice you can make is to eliminate some of the work altogether by firing some of your customer base. This means your overall sales COULD dip below their current levels, but what I typically see is that profits will increase when overhead reductions are calculated into the equation. In reality, removing specific equipment will not remove 50% of sales. Instead, it will be closer to the 20% - 30% range. While this is still significant, it will not matter as much IF you make overhead and workforce reductions to compensate.

Remember, being in business is not about who has the most sales. It's about who has the most money at the end of the day AFTER all expenses are calculated. If you can be MORE profitable on $1 million in sales instead of $1.5 million in sales why wouldn't you do that?

What about processes?

If you are not a business that relies on heavy equipment, then you are a business that relies on processes.

Like the exercise you performed to uncover your equipment needs, you must also decide if you have wasteful or antiquated processes that do not take advantage of today's technological changes.

The problem you will find is that it is easy to ignore wasteful processes in the same way it is easy to ignore how large an iceberg really is. If you were to view an iceberg in the ocean you would only be viewing about 10% of the total mass. The rest is hidden below the water's surface and we pay little attention to it. Like the iceberg, it is easy to not see (or ignore) wasteful processes because we only observe the slight inefficiencies. What we fail to uncover are the actual costs to our organization.

For example, a wasteful process of only ten minutes, if done a total of one hundred times a week by multiple people equates to 1,000 wasted minutes or almost seventeen wasted hours a week. Over the course of a year, that is 884 hours or **twenty two** wasted **WEEKS** in a typical 40 hour work week. Are you ready to waste over five months of process time because you allow the ten minute inefficiencies to continue? Always remember the iceberg affect!

Step Two: What People Do You Need?

Whether it's a change in equipment or a change in processes, there are always people attached. Many times people remain with us out of lack of proper management. In other words, they are hired and remain in their positions only because we have never gotten personally involved with them. We ignore their roles or their inefficiencies and after a while we keep them around because it's the path of least resistance.

While I'm not an advocate of blindly removing people who have been with you for years; I am an advocate of creating a better business and unfortunately this can involve the removal of workers. This has happened in every industry in the world at some point. Barrel makers were replaced by cardboard box manufacturers. Record player repair shops were replaced by audio tape player repairers and they too were eventually replaced as media went to CD format and eventually MP3. Change happens in EVERY business and while you should shy away from being on the bleeding edge of change, you MUST change (i.e. evolve) if you want to survive.

The choices you ultimately make about future workers should involve not only equipment and processes but skill-sets as well. As technology evolves, the need for different skill-sets evolves as well. What used to be 100% technical (i.e. processed by a human operator) may now be computer-driven and that may mean a different type of worker is needed. That's okay because this is a state of nature and as long as you don't fight it, you can make the next evolutionary step.

Finally, if you are hesitant to remove equipment / change processes / remove people, you need to give it a test drive before making the hard decisions. The best way to do this is to literally shut off a piece of equipment for thirty days and see how it impacts your production flow. Can the work be sent to another piece of equipment? Can it be done a completely different way? All of these tests can be made BEFORE you take the ultimate leap, and I highly suggest testing all changes before the equipment leaves the door. Just make sure you are giving it a proper test and a minimum of thirty days. Done correctly, this can be a major shift in bringing your business to the next level!

Step Three: What Space Do You Need?

It is virtually impossible to do Step Three until you have taken a hard look at Steps One and Two. You must make a decision about what equipment, processes and people will change before you can make a decision about space. Obviously, if you remove equipment and/or people you will not need as much space, but, that's just the beginning of the exercise.

The two key decisions that must be made as far as space is concerned are:

1. Cost of moving. If you decide to move from one location to another not only do you need to think about what space to eliminate, but you have to think about what TYPE of space you will need in the future. For example, today you may be in a higher priced retail space. In the future you may be better served by a lower cost industrial space.

Regardless, downsizing will require reorganizing hard assets at best and moving facilities entirely at worst. All of this requires a great deal of money that must be worked into your decision making process. Typically, the obvious costs such as moving the physical equipment are easily calculated, but the less obvious costs are forgotten or underestimated. These hidden costs often involve electrical requirements and even structural requirements as heavy equipment requires special flooring that can handle the loads. Don't just look at the obvious but look at the entire process when making your final decision!

2. Proximity to customers. Assuming you do decide to move to a new space altogether, how will your customers find you if you move off the beaten path? This of course ties back to your sales plan which should serve as a reminder that NOTHING in business can be observed from a myopic view.

Businesses are a complex system and every stage of a business's processes will affect another stage.

The best way to prepare for this challenge is to once again look at your top 5% customers who represent 50% or more of your overall sales. The only question to answer at this point is:

How did these customers find you in the first place?

This sounds simple but it is one of the most important (and overlooked) questions that could keep you from making a very poor decision. For example, if your top 5% customers found you because of the signage on your building, then you need to proceed with caution! Moving your business to a location that did not have visible signage could be catastrophic to your future growth. On the other hand, if your top 5% customers found you through sales activities (online or offline), then a move to cheaper space is not a bad decision.

The bottom line is to use all of the information at your disposal and to not make a hasty decision just to save money. Make sure your decision is helping you EVOLVE and not just play defense. You should be preparing yourself to play OFFENSE in a new and unique way that will allow you to stand out from the competition and add more money to your bottom line.

Step Four: How is Your Top 5% Customers Evolving to Emerging Technologies?

Finally, the decisions you make about your future are not always about you. In fact, you must acknowledge how outside forces might affect YOUR customers. You can plan for your future but you can't do so effectively without at least taking a peek at your customers' future.

In order to do this you must be aware of what is going on in your customers' lives. The best way to do this is to simply ask. After all, your top 5% customers should be comfortable with you and your business. They should see you as a valuable resource and as someone who has their best interests at heart. Use this equity to your advantage.

The best way to approach this is face to face with a scheduled appointment. The purpose of this visit is not to sell them anything but instead to start a conversation about how YOU can help THEM for years to come. You will need to uncover information such as:

- What technological changes are affecting your industry?

- How do you see your business evolving over the next five years? Ten years?

- What is your greatest opportunity for future growth?

- How has your business processes changed over the last five years? Ten years?

Answers to questions such as these will give you insight on where your customer has come from, and more importantly, where they are heading. This means you can plan your future based on their prediction of their future. But you must proceed with caution to do this effectively.

For starters, you can't take every word they say as gospel. In fact, some of their words will be hopes and dreams while others will be educated facts. What you are looking for are trends which means it is always better to ask more than one customer within each market niche. The more you ask the better, but always start from the top of your customer list and work down.

In terms of making decisions based on your customer interviews, you should not use them as your sole basis for change. Instead, look at your decision from a holistic view and always lean on facts before feelings. In other words, don't make a major business decision because only one customer says that "X" will probably happen in a couple of years. Do your research and get more facts before pulling the trigger on any major decision built upon customer comments. I've seen too many businesses go down a slippery slope solely based on a customer's unmet promises. Don't let that be you.

Wrapping It All Up

The concepts we have discussed will certainly work for your business because I observe them in hundreds of businesses I work with each and every year. They are built upon solid principles and not just "feelings." Like a great sports team, the fundamentals are what get you to the top on a consistent basis, and applying the 80/20 within the 20% in every facet of your life will help you to get there too.

What happens when you get off track?

This is bound to happen at some point or another because we are human and we will err from time to time. Therefore, all we can do is acknowledge the steps we took to get off the path and choose not to make them again. From there, I would go back to your original "Finding the 5's" exercise which is a great way to remind yourself of what brings you success the quickest. If the activity is not a "5," why are you spending time focusing on it?

Applying 80/20 to Your Life

Because the 80/20 within the 20% is a principle of life, we can also apply this to EVERY area outside of our business as well. We can take a look at things such as:

- What allows us to lose weight the quickest?

- What allows us to prepare for a sporting event the quickest?

- What allows us to be the best mom / dad / husband / wife / brother /sister the quickest?

- What allows us to build personal wealth the quickest?

- What allows us to get out of debt the quickest?

- And so on . . .

The best way to apply these principles to your life and not just your business is by starting with the "Finding the 5's" exercise. For example, if losing weight is your goal, do a "mind dump" of the ways in which you have lost weight the quickest. How often did you eat during the day? What exactly did you eat? Was exercise involved? If so, what kind?

By getting these activities out on paper you have a good start to the "Finding the 5's" process. From there, list your activities on the spreadsheet I provided and then rank these activities from 1 to 5, with 5 being the most effective. When you are finished, you will know exactly what allows <u>you</u> to lose weight quickly. After that, the rest is up to you to follow your personal blueprint until you achieve your weight loss goal.

Whether you are applying these principles solely in your business or in a combination of business and personal life areas, the results are up to you. Nobody can care more than the leader of the business and nobody can help you reach your goals if you are not willing to apply action to the roadmap you have built.

Now what are you going to do?

Finding out what matters most is hard, but doing something about it is even harder! Are you ready to reshape your business or are you going to let fear keep you from seeing the profits and time you deserve? The choice is up to you.

We are what we repeatedly do. Excellence, then, is not an act, but a habit

-Aristotle

Resources

www.ToddNuckols.com

To read the latest tips, tricks and techniques on the world of 80/20 go here to sign up for the free 80/20 newsletter.

www.ToddNuckols.com/Resources

All of the resources I mentioned in this book and recommend for your business are found at this page.

www.ToddNuckols.com/leaderbook

This is an example of a lead capture page with basic information.

www.ToddNuckols.com/FreeAnalysis

This is an example of a lead capture page with advanced information.

www.ToddNuckols.com/PPC

This is a list of courses that will teach you Pay Per Click advertising methods.

Index

Made in the USA
Middletown, DE
25 February 2017